COMMOTIONS

New Writing from the Oscar Wilde Centre

Trinity College Dublin

Staff

COMMOTIONS

Commotions gratefully acknowledges
the generous financial support of the School of English, TCD.

ISBN 10: 0-9555025-5-1
ISBN 13: 978-0-9555025-5-2

Typesetting by Anú Design.
Printed and bound by Betaprint, Dublin 17.

Commotions
Oscar Wilde Centre for Irish Writing
21 Westland Row
Trinity College Dublin
Dublin 2
Republic of Ireland

For information on the M. Phil. in Creative Writing at TCD
visit www.tcd.ie/OWC

Acknowledgments

The authors of *Commotions* would like to thank: Stephen Matterson and Brenda Brooks at the School of English, Trinity College Dublin; Lilian Foley at the Oscar Wilde Centre; as well as Deirdre Madden, George O'Brien, Paula Meehan, Tom Kilroy, Michael O'Loughlin, Michael Longley and Jonathan Williams. Without their support and encouragement this project would not have been possible.

Contents

Introduction

Commotions is an apt title for this book of fresh, affecting new writing from the students in the Oscar Wilde Centre at Trinity. Commotion, in the first place, is a notable term in the aesthetic vocabulary of the great American story-writer Katherine Anne Porter—someone known to the writers included in this volume. In an interview conducted for the *Paris Review* in 1963, Porter sought to explain how a story she'd written—"The Flowering Judas"—had first numinously announced itself to her when she was still a beginning writer. "And when I looked through that window that evening," Porter says, "I saw something in Mary's face, something in her pose, something in the whole situation, that set up a commotion in my mind." Another writer could've put different words to that resonant, wordless appeal: called it "a felt need for language;" or "a sudden tidal pull;" or simply "an inspiration." Porter's mental *commotion*—whatever it was—represented what she believed to be the first sensible signal from the outward world to the inward realm that something was "there," or at least could be put there by her, in response to, or in consequence of, or as a bright figment representing what she'd felt or imagined as a significant private immanence. (Motivation, we all know, begins to be a murky business when we try to make a precise science out of it.)

Porter was nearly forty when she published "The Flowering

Judas," in 1930. She was— like the writers in this anthology—still new to her vocation, having *lived* considerably more than she'd written through her youth (also true of some writers here). But her interview makes clear her belief that being acutely sensitized to the lurking, inchoate possibility of a story is an essential to any writer's kit, and may also be a sign by which one comes to detect if one is likely for the vocation *at all*. One might naturally wonder: Can I even be a writer if I lack such a commotion? Or, is the story or the poem a commotion's only evidence? Or, do all commotions feel the same? Or, finally, is all this just a lot of over-fine Ouija board foolishness Flaubert would've rolled around laughing about, whereas what writers need to do is shut up and write. These are "concerns" writers think and sometimes even worry about—and not just at the beginning of their writing lives, I'm forced to say.

This course in "detection" (asking, "Am I any good at this?") is the course currently being followed by the writers in "the Oscar." And this volume—the profit from most of one school-year spent writing—stands as their best writing-to-date, and also stands as the early evidence from which they'll try to determine how the whole scheme's going. The signs, I think you'll agree, are very good.

Commotion, of course, is a word that leads us other ways, too. These are bewildering times to be embarking on a writer's life— although Samuel Johnson probably said the same thing when he saw his play *Irene* performed in1749 (it wasn't even very good, but he still became Samuel Johnson). There's little use to rehearse the dour literacy figures, the downward-tending numbers in the book trade, the feral gleam in the publishers' eyes as they scan the horizon for blockbusters (rarely for short stories and villanelles). I've always told young writers—even in the blissfully-literate, pre-PlayStation days when I was a youth—that if you can talk yourself out of this line of work, you probably should. (I say the same thing to prospective brides and grooms.) After all, the chances of palpable success in either undertaking aren't very good. In both, you're likely to end up alone in a room with a book, pissed off and broke, with only your-self to blame. Though maybe that's a kind of commotion, in itself.

There's actually plenty of sound (and conflicting) evidence for any argument here. But it always comes down—as here—to what you've written and whether it's any good.

Still, if you just can't seem to turn it off, or push it away, or as Ogden Nash (one of *my* favorite poets) wrote, "leave it aside," then there's a brio to that commotion, too—a stirring in your middle parts that won't be stilled or denied (at least at first) and that demands a serious go be given. That's vivid, too. No? If you even once have such a feeling in your life you're lucky. Of course, in the faces of most beginning writers this kind of rare commotion doesn't always surface as a big, wholesome, ice-cream smile of good fortune. More often, in fact, it surfaces in a visage for which the word "distrait" finally finds an apt reference. But it's a precious commotion all the same, and must—by those who contain it—be recognized as such. Bad, funny, serious old Larkin wrote that "Deprivation is for me what daffodils were for Wordsworth." But need we doubt that a large stirring was there, a rushing commotion that inspired and sustained the writer and found its consequential evidence in literature?

But let's end this on a brighter note than deprivation. At the business end of any poem or story, *commotion* most importantly denotes the experience all imaginative writing intends for its readers. It's what all of us who do this work want our writing to engender, whether we're cozy admitting that or not. It's why we come out of the back woods, why we leave good-paying jobs as lawyers and middle-management fuss-budgets, why we (though not I) leave marriages behind, or puzzled lovers and squalling kids; why we climb the s toried stairs at the Oscar Wilde Centre, or toward some other dank abode, and hand our work around, and stew and brood when we don't hear words we like—and stew and brood even when we do. And why we ultimately publish it and—as here—ask an audience. Because we want what we've written to set a thrumming going. We want what we've written to do what Leavis said literature *should* do—renew sensuous and emotional life and somehow impart a new awareness for whoever reads it. Most of us are writers because we once sat down and read something that excited just such a commotion in us. And because of it, we came to think: Maybe I could do that for someone. Set such a commotion going. Maybe there's a life to that. A calling. Art doesn't become beautiful until it escapes its maker and reaches, in this case, its reader. So here, then, is what these new writers have set free for us now. And in the pages that follow I believe you'll find writing that indeed is beautiful, that sets a commotion alive in you all by itself, and that responds stirringly, sometimes audaciously, to literature's privileged call.

Richard Ford
February 22, 2009
East Boothbay,
Maine

Andrew McEneff

The Garden and the Weeds

I woke with a fright. My dad was banging on my bedroom door. It's nearly two in the afternoon, he said. Get up! It was all a bit sudden, I thought, a bit extreme. He really did pound the door with his fist. It was hard not to notice how manic he got when the sun was out. It was like he was burning up with ways to keep me occupied. All I wanted to do was lie in. I had been at a beach party the night before. I needed my sleep.

From my bed I could see the perfect circle of the sun through my curtains. He could have just let me be, I thought, as I rolled around in my bed. I tossed off the blankets and flipped them over, hoping that they'd be cool. My dad called again from downstairs. I didn't want to get up but already I was uncomfortable, awake and aware. My mouth was dry. I whipped off the blankets and they fell to the ground. He wasn't going to leave me alone all summer if I didn't get a job. I'm only fifteen I kept telling him, I can't work, well, not legally anyway—but it just didn't register. For as long as I'd be around the house, his house, he would think of something for me to do. There were no excuses. I looked at the long, dim white doors of my closet and thought about it for a second. I saw myself sneaking into the closet and closing the door quietly behind me, but there were no real places in my room to hide. And besides, he'd always find me.

I reckoned that my dad could have lied about the time, it might only be ten or eleven o'clock; it felt early. I looked down at my feet. There was sand on my toes, little tiny crystals and sparkles of the night before. I remembered I had chased Katie through the dunes and kissed her in the caves. She had said she was sorry that she'd kissed me, that she'd made a mistake and liked Mark more, but I didn't care. I stayed behind and just listened to the waves. I stared at my feet and the sand on them as though at a beautifully captured photograph of all of us together on the beach. The sands of love I said then, quietly to myself. Then I got up and didn't feel as bad as I thought I would. I was a bit unsteady on my feet and felt strangely taller than usual. At the window I pulled back the curtains and hissed like a vampire, turning away and shielding my eyes from the sunlight. If I had actually burst into flames, I supposed, at least it would have been funny.

In the kitchen I stood in my boxer shorts and t-shirt and ate a bowl of cereal. My sister and my mother were out. Dad was outside. I could hear the ladder being dragged against the side wall, then being moved and clattered around to the back of the house. The tiles were cool under my feet. Tired of standing, I leaned against the fridge and ate the rest of my cereal. Some of the hair hanging over and around my mouth was wet with milk. I opened the dishwasher, put my bowl and spoon in and closed it.

My dad walked past the kitchen window. He was wearing his white sunhat and tinted glasses. He was coming for me. He came in the back door and called my name. When he turned into the kitchen, he stopped and stood looking at me. His grey and white beard made his face look redder than it actually was. He was sweating. His tiny little eyeballs glared at me through his tinted glasses. He looked like some ballistic DIY commando. In one hand he clutched a paintbrush and a hammer; he had a dirty paint-speckled rag in the other. The bristles at the top of the brush were all stained with white paint. Get some clothes on he said, you're doing the weeding today.

It was hot in the back garden. I watched my dad as he pulled and dragged his way deeper into the shed. He had already begun clearing it out. There were bikes and hoses, planks, shovels and rakes and paint-cans in front of the shed. Inside the shed my dad grabbed something, pulled at it and it fell over. I heard it break and he cursed and started clambering past a bag of sails, some canisters and the lawnmower. When I thought about it I found that while my dad does clear the shed out every now and then, he never really seems to throw anything away. There was an old table umbrella lying across an even older barbecue set near the shed door. He'd replaced them both, years before, but there they were, still there. The umbrella was rotten and discoloured with mildew. They'll probably be stored back away again neatly, I thought to myself, smiling. It was the bi-annual shed-shuffle.

I stepped through the doorway of the shed. It was cool inside and smelled of cut grass, petrol, wood and rust. It was the shaded home of spiders' webs, dead flies and woodlice; the dangerous world of saws, blades, paints and white-spirit; things I pretended not to know about or even see. Here, he said, giving me a trowel, a hand rake and shears. Wait a sec, I said, my hands are full, and I went back outside and dumped the tools on the grass. The hand rake fell and pierced the soil like desperate fingers. I went back into the shed, my arms outstretched, ready for more. That's all you'll need, he said. He turned around and wiped his brow. I moved backward as he came towards me and we both stepped out of the shed. Get started over there, he said, pointing to the darkest corner of the garden. Weed the flowerbeds and cut back anything that's overgrown. I could see that he had just hosed the garden and I heard water dripping and smelled the sinking, dark earth. I have to pick up a fountain in the garden centre, so I'll be gone for a bit. We're going to put it at the back there, he said and pointed over to the brighter corner of the garden where the hanging yellow-green leaves, the purple and orange and white flower petals lazed in the sun.

It was cold in the shade where I was, down on my hands and knees. I decided to weed first and cut back the tangling branches around the wall after. I looked forward to using the shears. They were just huge garden scissors. Snip-snip-snip. Chop-chop-chop.

That was going to be more satisfying than the weeding. I dug at the weeds; I trowelled them; I raked and twisted them but still I had to pull them out by the roots with my hands. They stung and cut my hands and fingers. I should have worn gloves but I didn't and the weeding itself eventually distracted me from the pain. It was almost hypnotic. See the weed, dig it, twist it and pull. See the weed, dig it, twist it and pull. It had its own momentum. I liked being in among the dripping leaves, the flowers and the damp, wet earth. I picked a worm out of a clump of muck. It had been a while since I'd held a worm, and it writhed against my fingers. It was thick, slimy and I could feel it spasm when I cupped it in my hands. Its body was brown, red and swelling; it was blind. I felt it wriggle again in my hands. I liked it and still it felt disgusting.

There were a lot of weeds to get rid of. I piled them up on a plastic bag behind me. The day before yesterday my dad had me rake the stones in the driveway. That had been the most meaningless chore of them all. As I raked the stones, I had told him that I knew the myth of Sisyphus and asked him if he did. No, but I'm sure you'll tell me all about it, he'd said, forcing his foot down on the shovel and turning over some soil. I guess my dad only cares that I do the chores to prove to my mother that they still have control over me. That's what I've taken to be the meaning of the little tasks he has me do, nothing more. And I like to let them think that they still control me. I help them foster that illusion because sometimes I feel sorry for my parents. They must worry about having a son like me. So I let them have me from time to time. I submit.

My back and my hands were sore and aching so I took a break from the weeding. I sat on the grass, rested back on my hands and looked around. All the colours of the plants and flowers and trees were really coming out in the sun. I looked down at my dirty knees. With the nail of one of my dirty fingers I scratched the side of my neck. When my right hand went back down on the grass, I looked at it. It was dirty with soil and I could see the red little scrapes and cuts from the weeds. Grass covered most of the fingers. The little finger was almost completely covered up in the grass, buried almost. It was weird, I thought, being buried. All that flesh that goes to rot underground. Only bones and skulls left over. I didn't like the thought of it. Everyone I knew who had died had been cremated: three grandparents. They all seemed to prefer that way. Buried or burnt. Neither really appealed to me. I looked at my little finger and moved it in the grass. I pressed it down so that the nail and the top of it went into the cold muck, under the grass. I stopped and pulled it back out. It looked dirty and small.

I tried to think what the little right finger was really for. I looked at it up close and then, at a distance, with my arm outstretched I looked at it again. It didn't seem to do much. I could put a ring on it, but I could put a ring on any finger. It did give a nice precise pick of the nose. I liked that but so could the little finger on my left hand. I cleaned my right finger off on my shorts and picked my two nostrils with it, first the right, then the left. Then I cleaned the left little finger and did the same, first the left, then the right. It was just as good and pretty much the same. I wrote with my left hand so that didn't matter, but just in case I mimicked holding a pen with my left hand, then with my right and determined that the little finger had nothing to do with balancing a pencil or pen in either hand. It was when I gripped things that I noticed the little finger made more sense. I had more of a grip on things. I gripped the trowel in my right hand with my thumb and four fingers, then with my thumb and three fingers. There was a definite difference all right, but whether or not it was considerable I couldn't tell. It was the same when I made a fist. The fist seemed stronger, harder, with all four fingers clenched and yet that wasn't enough to convince me either. I don't even know if I thought about it properly or why the idea came into my head, but it seemed, in an instant, that I had made up my mind. I grabbed my trowel and dug a little hole.

I looked around and made sure no one had come back into the house before I moved closer to the flowerbed and I put my little finger between the blades of the shears. It was strange but when the two blades pressed against my little finger, the sensation seemed familiar. Fingers must expect it somehow, I thought, or have a memory of being cut off. I lined up the blades carefully. This was just something that certain people chose to do, I told myself. I took a slow, deep breath and looked away. The blades quickly clicked together. I yelped and let out a little whimper. I felt the blades go right through and meet. I couldn't believe it. I did it. But the little stub of flesh on the gravel path seemed odd and out-of-place when I saw it. Then I felt the blood come out of the top, as if it was being sucked out of me by a tiny suction pipe. The sight of the blood made me feel sick and suddenly I felt light and airy as though I was fading away. I was really bleeding. I held the bleeding stump of my little finger tight with my left hand.

For some reason I hadn't anticipated the pain. But at the same time I didn't register the full pain of the cut. With my thumb and main finger on my right hand I picked up the bloody top of my little finger. It looked so small. For a second I wanted to bite the little fingernail on it. I dropped it into the hole and covered it with soil with my feet. When it was covered over completely and the patch of ground looked like the rest of the flowerbed, I started to feel afraid, a bit unreal, like my body wasn't mine. I ran back into the house. The thrill of the rush and novelty of what I had done was wearing off, rapidly. I was seriously injured, I thought, and I had done it all to myself. When I was inside I looked around for something to use, for something to help me. I felt like maybe I was going crazy and I started to panic. I thought I was going to die. All I could hear in my head were words like veins, veins and arteries, arteries and the loss of blood results in death.

In the utility room I washed my cut-off finger and took deep breaths. It stung and bled out more into the sink. My blood was bright red. From the presses I found an old piece of twine and wrapped it really tight just underneath the stump. I couldn't look at it but it felt like it was a clean cut. Nothing was left hanging or dangling. I tied the twine in a knot with my left hand and teeth. I was thinking practically. Everything was making sense again. I was doing my best to save myself, to survive. When I tied the knot up with my teeth, the cut came right up under my eye. When I glimpsed it up close, I retched. I could see the tender pink and red flesh, the little white bone inside. My stomach clenched as I vomited up chunky bits of milky cereal into the sink. I washed my mouth out from the tap and turned it off. From the clotheshorse I grabbed a dark brown towel and covered my wound. Everything was cool and dim and calm in the kitchen and, at the sink, with a steadier hand, I poured myself a glass of water. My head felt light and dizzy again and I was sweating down my back. My ears hurt a little too, as if they had been ringing. I gasped after I drank back the water and filled it up again immediately. I didn't want to pass out. I had to stay conscious. I took the phone from the charger and the glass of water and went and sat at the kitchen table. I looked out at the garden from the window of the patio door. My brow was cold and sweaty. I concentrated on my breathing and tried to remain calm.

But I was going to have to explain it; I had to think of an excuse. An accident of course, but I had to figure out how, how it happened, how it could have happened. I had a feeling that they weren't going to believe me, no matter what I said. I'd get in so much trouble. They'd know I did it to myself. The thought of getting caught cutting off my little finger made me feel even worse. There was no reason at all for doing it. They'll kill me, I thought. I had to think of something to say.

After a while the sun came out more brilliantly and lit up the garden again. It looked so warm outside. I could have dozed off or slept a little because I wasn't thinking of any excuses any more when I came around again on the chair. I was tired, almost tranquil. My breathing had steadied and I wasn't sweating or feeling sick any more. I looked over at the shaded part of the garden, where my dad had hosed the plants. I felt drugged and relaxed. The dark leaves still dripped at the place where I had been weeding. I was looking exactly at the spot where I knew I planted my little finger. I knew exactly where it was, between the fuchsia and the honeysuckle, under and to the right of the long stem of the front yellow tulip. It was in there, hiding in the earth. I could feel it, cold and enclosed in the dark. I couldn't make up my mind if I had buried my little finger or planted it. I thought about that for some time while I looked out the window. I soon realized that you can't plant a body and you don't bury a seed. Some things grow and some things decay. Humans decay in the ground, nothing else. They mould and rot and decay. They don't grow there. It was a very sad thought. I didn't want to think about it any more.

I sat at the kitchen table and looked out at the tiny patch of soil in the flowerbed. I hoped something would sprout up all of a sudden from my finger and surprise me. I didn't feel weak or faint any more when I thought about that. It was summer and the garden was inviting. I stood up when I heard a car approach. My strength was back. I could hear the tyres come around closer, toward the front door, crushing over the pebbles and stones of the driveway. My dad was home.

I moved closer to the window and looked out into the garden. I knew I was being unrealistic, even crazy, but I hoped for it regardless. I wanted to see something weird, something beautiful and completely alien grow up out of my little right finger. I stared at the flowerbed and tried to picture all the things that it might become.

Erin Rhoda

White Silhouettes

We drifted through the city
as two mourning doves might spend their lives:
flitting, halting, parting for minutes
but always nearby.
Snowflakes fell as night gathered,
and we strolled cautiously
on new ice. We were engulfed
by the stones of buildings
and a banjo player's song.
In the nightfall
we went down
and down farther
to the water and the boats.
We climbed aboard a yacht,
unmanned and brooding in the waves,
and sat on the upper deck
in the last splinters of sun,
while the clouds spilled snow
upon our wings.
It was visible in the night,
smoothing the cars and buildings
to their basic forms. I imagined
us encased, two bumps
on a stranger's boat. I never really
loved you. Still I thought of us
years later in rocking chairs
on our front lawn, wrapped
in blankets and becoming pure white.
Falling snow isn't silent but a whispering.

Leftovers

She unclipped her belt where she stood
in the room of dust, and he looked at her,
still wearing his coat and hat.

They were in the cottage by the lake,
and the loons had just flown south
for the winter. The sheets in her parents' bed
were cold like raw meat against her back and legs.

They brushed out the mice droppings and sand,
and she lost her virginity there. It was the day before
he left for Iraq. In the kitchen back home,

the tomatoes grew soft and liver-spotted,
and later she'd cook summer squash, overripe.
She'd slice the rind to scoop out the seeds, hard like teeth,
cup them in her palms, and lovingly mash them

into her face. She'd remember the flakes of his skin
that came off in her hand that night, loosened by his hours
under the sun and rising from his back

like the veils of brides. They found the dead skin
in the sheets in the morning and picked it all up

and threw it away, and like that he was gone.

Hope Seeds

I pressed my cheek to my mother's back
as she carried me into the bush outside Kumasi,
the cloth pulled tight and knotted beneath her breasts,
a machete in her hand, an empty bowl balanced
atop her cropped hair. Her pulse sounded in my ears
like the throb of a distant city.
She piled the green, ripe cocoa pods
until she built a steeple on her head.

Later she spread the pulp
on the cement where it sweated
until the time was right to take the seeds
and dry and rake them in the sun.
Then she took my hands,
and we walked barefoot over the seeds
to soften them. This is how I learned to walk.
"If you walk on cocoa seeds," she said,
"no path will be too rough." She said,
"My daughter is cocoa; cocoa, my daughter,"
and I thought that anything left in the sun
would become like the sun: the beans
that turned golden, the white laundry
that bleached as it dried on the rocks.

Like spiders we made our home
facing the rising light,
but growing up my skin got darker,
and one day my neighbor—
he stretched me out—the floor familiar—

his sweat and alcohol crushing my breath,
the stain a spreading shadow.
Night gathered, and the dew
dripped from my mouth.
Beyond me women pounded cassava
in their wooden bowls, and somewhere
my mother wrenched the chocolate fruit
from the tree, the oblong pods
a force driving her into the ground.
Sunlight takes its turn on every wall.

Following Footsteps

It was April. I'd be born in May,
and my mother stood at the starting line
of the Boston Marathon, her long hair

the color of old hay. My mind doesn't remember
the beat of her footsteps, but my body does.
Four years later I sprinted, streaming song

down our road beneath umbrellas of orange leaves.
She was all flannel, humming off tune. In the winter
she slathered Vaseline on her face. Returned

from running, her eyelashes were frost daisies,
and the ice chips falling from her red scarf
to the floor were chimes. We ran a race

when I was twelve, and my sides cramped til
I was green and bent like a willow branch,
but she stayed with me, urging me on. We crossed

the line last, shoulder to shoulder, but they marked her
one second slower than me. I finished my first marathon,
and she wasn't there. I was across the world beneath

a violet sky in a stadium that shivered with butterflies.
I sat, my hands cupping my knees, fragile like
sand dollars; they might have been her hands.

ERIN RHODA   17

Years later, the house as calm as cold milk,
I climbed under the blue sheets with my mother
who tucked her nose beneath my cheek. All sinew

and lung, her frame as small as a child's,
her breathing slowed in the rhythm of sleep.

In My Doorway

The clouds are an ocean before me
as I stand in the doorway of my home in Maine.
I see this view every day of my life.
The fields, trees, and sky
extend to everything and nothing.
It's sometimes all I need, in darkness and daylight.

I'm here when I learn about my friend.
A few months ago above his hospital bed
on the white board he'd written, "I want to die,"
in his boyish scrawl, and I don't know why
no one erased it. He smashed a chair against the window,
trying to escape, which was unlike him,

but maybe we never know the insides of people.
I'm already forgetting him and the way his lazy eye
roamed when he listened. The time he sailed
across the lake to surprise me, and I hadn't been home.
How he greeted people with hugs
and planted the rows of his gardens in spirals.

The night before, he and his girlfriend made burritos,
and he packed his with loads of beans.
The next morning as she left for work
he went into the bathroom, and she said,
"Have fun stinking up the bathroom!"
That was the second to last thing she said,

the last being, "I love you." That night she found
six orange sticky notes, saying he couldn't love her more
than he hated himself. It was his mother's birthday; he carved her
a wren from wood but didn't come for dinner; they found him
by the ocean with a gun and no more heart. There's nothing more
to say. He was a boy who was sick and he died.

There will be a death, too, for standing in my July doorway,
a death for these fields, trees, and sky eventually,
and a death for every goodbye.
And what will remain is unknown.
Maybe it won't be that bad, not existing—
at least then there won't be questions.

The Red House

There's a silence about the red house. As I walk up the front stoop, through the porch and into the kitchen, the hush pries into closed spaces. My parents have been cutting wood for winter, canning hot peppers and freezing corn, taking care of the sheep, and doing everything they are used to: working full-time, going to church, playing violin. Only somehow today is stiller. My brothers are away at college, and the house is larger.

Years ago, my youngest brother Jason, my mother, father, friend Melissa, and I sat at this dinner table in the kitchen. We waited for Adam, the middle child, to arrive so we could eat. He was bringing his girlfriend home for the first time, and we had made a feast of home-grown turkey, gravy, stuffing, potatoes, carrots, and five-cup salad.

By 8 p.m. we were tired of waiting and decided to play a joke on them. My father quickly drove his truck behind the barn, so they wouldn't think he was home. We then turned off all the lights in the house and sat at the dinner table in complete darkness.

"We should do this more often," my father quipped. "Now I don't need to look at the lot of you!"

"Paul!" My mother scolded him as he tried to reach for her in the darkness, and she playfully slapped his hands. We controlled our laughter when Adam's car sounded on the dirt driveway, and he and his girlfriend walked through the front door. It took them a moment to turn on the light, and when they did they gasped at the sight of us filling the kitchen, a turkey spread on the table. Adam's girlfriend covered her mouth with her hands as we shouted "Surprise!" and my mother quickly rose to give her a hug. My father sat at the table, looked at Adam's expression of shock and mild amusement, and laughed so hard the dog began barking. His laughter continued, loud and high, and we giggled along with him until eventually everyone was in hysterics, my mother snorting, Adam's girlfriend's laughter high like a bell.

Maine's light is different from other places. It's whiter, thinner. It's slower, too. It lets people look at it. The nights are different as well: they're colder and clearer, with stars bright like bones. The moon rises and sets beyond the front stoop, as if it's the sun.

We liked being in darkness, it seems, or maybe we were most active at night because Maine's long winters force an early sunset. With my brothers and I at school and my parents at work during the day, we spent the most time with each other after the sun went down, after the chickens were fed, homework was done, and the fire was made in the cellar. The red house is so far from light pollution that it's possible to have complete darkness. It's a half-hour drive from the grocery store and hospital, and there are no nearby houses in sight.

It was spring, and I had just returned to the red house from shopping. My parents were away on a hiking trip, but Jason and his friends were home, watching TV in the living room and eating lasagne my mother had made before she left. They didn't know how loud they were. I called out to them, "Hey, where's Olivia?" and they didn't hear me at first. I marched in and asked again, "Where's the dog?"

Jason glanced at me and said, "She's outside," and then continued jabbing his finger into a girl's side; she sat next to him on the couch, yelping. Another friend was doing a headstand on the couch, her dinner abandoned on the side table, precariously close to the edge.

I yelled for Olivia outside in the darkness, but she didn't come. She was an Australian Border Collie, a very smart dog, and she always came when called. I called her again and again. Jason heard me yelling and came outside with his friend Derek. They hollered for Olivia, too, and I strode down the road, looking in the ditches in case she'd been struck by a car. I walked around the house, still calling, and checked the barns. She was gone.

After ten minutes of shouting, Jason and Derek went back inside. I tried a different tactic. I stood in the front yard and just listened. There were some crickets but mostly silence. Faintly, I heard something like whimpering coming from the backyard. I rushed around the house and followed the sound, which led to our underground sewage tank.

The wooden boards that used to cover our sewer had fallen in, and below was Olivia, swimming in a dense, dark liquid waste. The stench was overpowering, but I told Olivia I had found her and she'd be all right. I lay down and tried to reach her, but the pit was too deep. I told her not to worry, that I'd be right back, and ran to the house to get Jason, roaring, "I found her! Come help me! Quick!"

Jason and his friends rushed outside, and we gathered around the sewer as Olivia struggled below, splashing at the sides, trying to get out. She cried up at us with little whining noises, too tired to bark. The smell was like raw meat left in a hot car for a week.

"What do we do?" I asked Jason. "Should we get a ladder?"

I ran to the barn to grab a ladder, and carried it back on my shoulders, still running. As I set it down, Jason's friend Derek, who was larger than me, reached into the sewer. He latched his grip to the scruff of Olivia's neck and yanked her up, while Jason held onto Derek's legs. She flopped to the ground like a fish, and we were caught between laughing and vomiting. Derek's front and his arms were layered in feces, and the smell was so strong we gagged. Olivia tried to shake off in front of us, and we ran away, shouting at her to stop. She was terrified and kept her tail between her legs and her head low. I told her it was OK, that she was safe. She rolled in the grass and licked at her paws.

I coaxed her to the front of the house, where the hose was, and tried to make her still so I could wash her down. She was petrified of the water and kept trying to run away, but I held her gently and got off as much of the sewage as possible. I noticed her feet were bleeding badly, and she kept licking them. She must have scratched them trying to get out of the sewer. I imagined she had thought she was going to die in that murky, sordid dump.

Her paws left gobs of blood on the floor as I urged her into the house and to the bathroom. I filled the bath with water and set her inside, pouring pots of warm water over her head and body. I soaped her black fur repeatedly with shampoo and conditioner, rubbing at the stench, my arms covered in waste and blood. Outside, the boys closed the sewer with fresh planks and rocks.

I washed Olivia for hours, and still the smell remained. I dried her with towels and a hair dryer, and I put ointment on her paws and wrapped them in rags. After she lay down on her dog bed, I wiped the bathroom of the blood and feces and took a shower. Still, I was not clean. I sat with Olivia and rubbed her fur to comfort her, even though the smell lingered, and the next day I brought her to the veterinarian for antibiotics. She would be fine, they said.

As I enter the kitchen, Olivia rushes to meet me, her backside twisting uncontrollably with her tail. She turns her face back and forth in front of me and does a little side dance as I tell her what a good girl she is and rub her head smooth.

My parents are good greeters, too. My mother says, "Ohhh, you're home!" and hugs me, her wiry body slightly smaller than my own. My father grins and dives toward me for a bear hug, twisting me up in his arms. I'm always surprised at them, how they never stop wanting me home. They clean the house and cook special foods: chili made with everything from our garden, Swedish pancakes called *platta*, or baked beans deluxe with pickles and olives. We talk about work, about my brothers at college, and they ask about my friends.

I wonder if they have changed or if I'm the one who has grown quiet. They are as I remember, and the house is the same. I think maybe we are losing things to fill the stillness, space, and darkness of this place. It's easy to drown in solitude. We used to be the light and loudness. We used to be young.

When it's time to say goodbye, my mother's eyes fill up, and my father hugs me more gently. I bend down to pat Olivia, and they press packaged food into my hands and tell me to drive safely and come back soon. We are always like this, but I know they will leave one day. We all do. I softly close the door and amble outside to my car. I could walk this path blind, but my mother, her worn and wrinkled finger at the switch, turns on the outside light.

Nicola Flynn

Memories of the Imagination

(an excerpt)

The urban streetscape Thom Hargadon is driving through soon gives way to narrow country roads, bounded by loose stone walls and fraying hedges. He is almost past Carrowmore before he sees it. From the road, the megalithic cemetery is just one more green field in an ongoing sequence. At the last minute, he notices incongruous scaffolding and, slowing, peering, he judges it is installed across an earth mound deep at the field's centre. A dolmen comes into view on the opposite side of the road, lurching from a hillock that has been cut back when the route was widened. The road appears to have been driven right through the heart of this megalithic site. He has a confused sense of history being physically evident here, while at the same time all meaning and sensibility has become hopelessly confused. He starts to feel depressed. The places the landlady has pointed out to him—*Culleens, Carrowmore, Knocknarea, Culleenamore*— no longer seem exotic or poetic. Once they had real meaning, they were evocations of culture, history, topography. With the passing of each generation, their true sense has been slipping away unacknowledged, a fragment of the past poking up incongruously through the fabric of the present.

He is parking the car when a text comes through and he grabs the phone but it is not from Sarah. Instead, there is an apology from Dalberg, postponing their meeting until after lunch. In Boston it is too early for Sarah to be awake yet anyway. As he holds the cell, he sees himself drawing her into his arms in the early morning, as he often did, kissing her sleeping face. 'I love you,' he would whisper, believing then that it was everything they needed. 'I love you too.' Her breath would be warm on his skin.

He gets out of the car. He can at least make a start on collecting background colour for his story. As he crosses the field, the scaffolding resolves itself into a structure bridging the dig. Close up, the monument is a huge rounded heap. Before the excavation began, it must have been all grassed over. A segment of its mantle has now been cut and peeled back, revealing the rough stone pile of the ancient cairn. *A visible evocation of the process of going back in time*. He begins to formulate the article in his mind. The entrance is revealed, a mysterious dark space framed by two stone slabs and a massive lintel.

The scaffolding stretches like a bridge across a deep trench that has been dug out through a cross-section of the monument. A man in a red T-shirt is working on the entrance to the mound. When Thom reaches the doorway he can see that the sward has been cut away at ground level, and all the grassy turf bricks form a miniature satellite mound a little distance away. The man in red turns out to be a research student of Dalberg.

"I help with the dig, but my work also looks at the social context."

"Do you have much to go on?"

"Not in the sense you mean, I think. Obviously, there is nothing written, no oral tradition. One must accept we can never truly know the past because we are always looking back at it—from the future, but also through all the futures there have been in the meantime, as it were."

"So how do you get over that problem?"

"You don't try to get over it. Actually, my method is to keep it in mind as I work. You accept what you do not know, yet you try to understand. No matter how much research I do, at some level what I deal with is what this monument signifies to us now."

"That sounds like a bit of a riddle."

"Yes—here, take this." The young archaeologist has picked up a small length of bone which he puts into Thom's hand. "Now you are holding the hand of someone who was alive four thousand years ago."

The bone is dark grey, almost black; damp and cold from its contact with the ground. It is a light weight on his palm. He thinks it would be more effective as a photograph than it is in reality, and says so.

"You are probably right. There is that contradiction again. We need to search out the evidence, but the only human connections possible are made in the imagination, and that works better from a distance."

•

After the visit to the site, Thom still has two hours to kill. He feels unsettled, in need of a walk. Grey clouds are gathering on the horizon, but he judges it will be some time before there is any danger of rain. Culleenamore is not significant enough to merit a signpost. He reaches it by dint of asking for directions at a gas station convenience store, where he buys himself a sandwich and a Coke. He asks first for Cullenbeg, but the young teenager behind the counter has not heard of it.

The beach has a pale beauty that strikes him as primal and raw. A wind blowing in off the sea moves restlessly through the long bent grasses. He strides out along it, relishing the physicality of walking. Here and there a sandy cliff tells of the corrosive power of the sea, and lays bare the dune's fragile network of plant roots. Three boys are having a kickabout, taking it in turns to defend a makeshift goal marked by stones. As he passes, the ball misses its mark and scuds across the sand towards him. Thom traps and returns it with an able touch that wins him a wave of acknowledgement. A whole summer was spent honing that particular ability. He would have preferred to work on his basketball skills in the hope of making the school team but his father had come out into the yard with a soccer ball. Another year it was jumping over hurdles, made by his father out of saplings he referred to as *buartree* sticks. He urged Thom on enthusiastically, using laundry pegs to attach the hurdle across the supports. But the training came to an abrupt end when Thom protested that the bar was raised too high. His childhood belief that he would become a star athlete finally died that summer. Adolescence was already on the horizon, and the next years were spent in the private personal pursuits of that age. The developing rift with his father seemed like an advantage then.

Thom moves farther down the beach. Ahead of him, a woman is walking a dog. Now and again, she throws a piece of driftwood out to sea for the dog to fetch. The sky has continued to darken, and suddenly there is rain, not soft like the day before, but in heavy drops that rattle off his windbreaker, and begin soaking into his trousers. He starts running up the beach to where a cliff with a grassy overhang offers shelter. The woman with the dog reaches it just ahead of him.

"Down Prince, down!" She calls out too late, and has to haul her companion away from Thom. "Oh dear, he will do that. Down, *get down*, Prince." She is older than he thought, probably in her seventies, with grey straight hair cut into a fringe.

"I hope you are not afraid of dogs?"

Her voice has a precise quality, an Irish accent overlaid, he guesses, with an English one. Curious, he makes conversation. To draw her out, he mentions his own putative connection with the area.

Yes, she has been in England for forty years, returning this summer to live in the old family home in Culleenamore.

As they talk, the dog sits between them watching the rain, the end of his tail thumping on Thom's shoe. The old lady keeps one hand on his collar.

"Retirement," she remarks regretfully, "seemed to creep up unbeknownst to me." But in many ways she was lucky, fortunate to be so hale and hearty at her age. "Your health is your wealth, isn't it?"

Listening, Thom is reminded of his father, whose tendency was to revert to the language of his youth when at his most emotional.

How could you think you would get away with this unbeknownst to me? was what he had flung at Thom, in the incident over the sneakers. But also *Go for it, that's the good gossoon,* he had called out as encouragement while they worked on the *buartree* jumps, delighted with him, Thom had believed at the time.

"Have you ever heard of somewhere named Cullenbeg?" he asks her as she falls silent.

"Cullenbeg; no, I don't think so. Oh dear, I left here a long time ago you know, and memories fade, I'm afraid. There was a place named Cull*een*beg I seem to remember, just along the road from here. And, actually, there were a family of Hargadons living there at one time. I was just a small child. Do you think there could be a connection?" She peers out at the sky. "Look, the rain has stopped. We can walk up the beach together, and I can point you in the right direction."

"You know, I didn't really expect this. Does anyone live there now? Are there any Hargadons left?"

"No, no. It was a sad story. When the mother and father died, there were only two still living in the house—a brother and a sister, and then the sister died. It was not too long after that, I would say, that the boy left. He walked away from the house one day it was said; just left it and everything in it."

"Everything?"

"Yes, everything. How could he take it with him? But there wouldn't have been very much. People were poor then. Even clothes and shoes were handed down, so there wasn't a lot to pack up." She looks at him, as if to check how he is receiving this. "Maybe he sold anything good and brought some small things he cared for. I never heard about that."

The old lady turns to look for the dog, who has been running ahead of them as they walk back towards the road. Thom whistles, picks up a stone and throws it for him.

"My father was only seventeen when he left. He died last year." He tries to look backwards, to make the tense middle-aged man of memory morph into the expectant teenager of 1936. There are no photographs from that period, nor for the next decade or more, until around the time his mother and father met. Then there is only one, of his father in his thirties, still gangly like a boy, but with his dark curls already thinning. He was squinting and grinning half-shyly, half-quizzically at the camera. They were said to be alike, he and his father. Thom thinks of a picture taken on his seventeenth birthday. He is smiling, outwardly confident anyway, his curly hair tamed to a thick fringe, with long sideburns in a fashionable style that his father objected to.

"I'm so sorry. What was his name?"

"Thomas. I was named after him."

"Oh. This boy was Jimmy, I think. As I told you, I was very young at the time. He might have been TJ, which could be Thomas James, you know. That was quite common."

"My father never spoke of those times…of his past. He said you could only go forward; that you shouldn't be looking back."

"There's a lot in that. Don't we make the history ourselves? We live it and then we tell it. History can be whatever you want it to be. Those were cruel times and he was starting a new life, it seems to me, a new beginning, wiping out the old. He would have wanted you to be free of all that."

They have come to the end of the beach, and Thom gives her his arm for support across the shingle.

"The house is still there, whatever is left of it," she says as they reach the road. "You could go to see it if you like. It's quite interesting for its own sake; it was built on a piece of no-man's land. The father didn't have any land of his own, you see, but once he was able to build this house overnight, then the authorities had to let him stay there."

"How could he do that?"

"He got his brothers and neighbours to help him."

"And where is it?"

"It's easy to find. It's on a bend on the shore road—built on a tri-angular piece left over between two other houses."

•

There is a narrow lane not far distant, as she has told him. He turns the little rental car into it and jolts along. There are few houses, and a green plume of grass gradually appears along the centre of the asphalt. He rounds the bend and in another fifty yards or so, the road has petered out. He turns, parks and gets out. The tide turned while he and the old lady were sheltering, and the sea is far up the beach here, the breeze raising stiff white tops across its chopped surface. A few pliant trees and tall bushes have been planted or have seeded themselves around the end of the road, where they give some shelter, and squarely facing them, set back somewhat into its own garden is a small, whitewashed building with a galvanised roof. This should be one of the cottages the woman said formed a side of the triangular site on which the Hargadon home was built.

Initially, he can see no trace of a structure on the corner. Walking towards it, the wind flapping at his raincoat, he hunches his shoulders and keeps his hands in his pockets. He is almost on it before he begins to make out the details. The front wall of the house, virtually on the line of the road, as she said, has long since fallen in. Grass, brambles and saplings have filled up the interior. One gable end remains, on the side nearest the whitewashed cottage, strengthened by the chimney going up through it. There is a broken hole where the fireplace once was. He pictures his father perhaps leaving here or, if not here, somewhere very like it, giving up everything that was familiar. *A new beginning.*

The old lady was wrong, he thinks. We can walk away from the past, but we need it too, because it explains who we are.

He stands there, watching, not sure whether this encounter should mean anything to him or not. Weak sunlight briefly lights the chimney where it rises above the vegetation, and reflects brightly off the whitewashed wall of the neighbouring cottage.

Bless the hearth and chimneys tall, let God's hope lie over all... As he turns for the car, the words come to him, like a benediction of sorts, though he does not see himself as a religious man. Driving back up the lane, he puzzles over it. There is a fragment of a tune attached to it, but he cannot get beyond this to the next line, or back to the beginning of the hymn, if it is a hymn, leading him to repeat it over and over again, annoyed at the memory lapse. Reaching the junction at the end of the lane, he has to stop and concentrate on his driving. The western flank of Queen Maeve's mountain rises steeply across the road in front of him. Both directions will take him to Carrowmore and his meeting with Dalberg—going right is more direct, but left would take him around by the bay, up the self-same estuary down which his father passed at the age of seventeen. He turns that way, negotiating carefully, reminding himself to keep to the left-hand side of the road.

He settles into a comfortable driving position, brakes for the sharp bend near Culleenamore. What he has been searching for comes to him. He remembers the words framed, hung on the wall of his bedroom, under a picture of an idealised thatched cottage, covered in climbing roses. *Bless this house, oh Lord we pray, make it safe by night and day.* He thinks he can recall his mother singing this to him like a lullaby. *Bless the roof and chimneys tall, let thy peace lie over all.* He had got that part wrong earlier. *Bless the door that it may prove ever open to joy and love.*

The road is high over the estuary now, with a view clear across the bay and out to the Atlantic where the sun, in another change of mood, has broken through the clouds. He realises he feels happy, a little exhilarated even, as if some weight has been lifted. He pulls into a lay-by overlooking the sea, and takes out his cell. He is going to call Sarah.

Sean Monaghan

Therapy

The Nacional Hotel, Havana, Cuba

"Calling the kids?" Paul asked.

Sitting at the study desk bathing in the lamp's yellow light, Gwen clipped back her blonde fringe, opened her white suit jacket and absentmindedly turned a page of *Harpers*.

"Yeah, you're right," Paul then said as if her silence was a practical affirmative. His undertone staggered along as if through mud. "It's early back home. Your sister will have brought them somewhere. Come to bed, baby. You're just in overdrive." The bed springs crowed under him.

Gwen wished there was something on TV besides CNN's despairing drumbeat of murder and Caribbean soaps that looked as if they'd been filmed by out-of-work porn crews. An hour before, through the spy-hole, she'd watched the rotund-fish-eyed-passing of a couple giggling about getting a taxi to *Hemingway's*. Gwen hadn't even been in a Cuban taxi because Paul had hired a huge hummer that in crumbling Havana looked like a tank built to protect five-star hotels.

Gwen glanced over at the lump snuggled beneath the blankets and thought of breast cancer. On the bedside table was a folder of newspaper clippings from a recent scandal about four Irish spinsters who had starved themselves to death in an incestuous orgy of weariness.

He'd promised that he wouldn't bring his research away on holidays.

She clicked open her gold wrist cuff. Gwen despised her husband's infantilising attempts to kind-uncle her into doing the 'right thing,' like 'calling the kids'. Recently she felt that life had suddenly lashed out against her, demonstrating that existence is not all about living— it's also about loss; endless, insatiable loss.

Gwen stared at the space above the bed as if all his drowsy sentences floated there. Then she opened the moisturiser from the complimentary-airline-goodie-bag and dunked her finger. For her, deflowering unspoiled ointments was as absorbing as popping bubble-wrap. Gwen leaned into the mirror as she rubbed the cream into her forehead. Her hair was styled into a blunt glossy bob with a soft side parting and her perfect nose was the perfect divisor for perfect green eyes. She wore just a hint of brown eyeliner and pale mocha-coloured lipstick. Opal earrings complemented her sallow skin. She was forty-seven and the jetlag made her feel every minute of it.

There was a distant drum sound. Gwen slipped behind the heavy blackout curtains and wiped a porthole of clarity through the condensation. The sculptured gardens were a black pit while the surrounding ramparts were floodlit; guards patrolled them like medieval knights with walkie-talkies. Beyond the ramparts, the Malecón promenade arced around the Straits of Florida. There were so many people on the promenade that they spilled onto Avenida de Antonio Maceo, halting traffic and waving placards as if trying to communicate with Gwen by semaphore from some folkloric land of salsa.

"Christ, turn the people *off*," Paul complained. He inhaled trapped air beneath the blankets and yawned. The room seemed to fill with age.

Gwen thought of the astonishing city view from her Dublin psychotherapeutic practice where she would ponder moral calculus while pawing her chin like a caricature of her idol, Freud. Affixed to the side of her computer were peel-off stickers of Tenniel illustrations from *Alice's Adventures in Wonderland*, while a crucifix nailed to the wall reminded her of a sanctity she'd sensed in mankind. An iron plaque entitled it *The Atheist on the Cross*. Gwen may have rejected religion but, unlike many others, she accepted the burden of her own existence.

Gwen turned from the window. "Think I'll pop down to the piano bar. A glass of wine will knock me out." She kicked off her leather slingback stilettos, stepped into satin sandals and took a roll of bills from her bag. "Back soon."

"How soon is soon?"

"One hour max," she murmured, as do those who must avoid speaking the truth.

Gwen strutted along the corridor. *Do not disturb* signs hung on most of the gilded iron handles. Between each room were marble tables supporting statues of condottieri and early twentieth-century Batista-era gouaches.

In the expansive lobby, stuccoed pillars were adorned with black and white photographs of important guests: Churchill, Sinatra, Marilyn, Hoover. Outside, beneath the porte-cochère, a porter held open the back door of a white Lada. Gwen stared up at the façade of the *Nacional*'s five-star hermetically sealed non-experience. Occasionally a figure passed a window like a shadow left out to play. She tried to work out which window her husband lay behind when the relevance of what she was doing hit her like the final line of a whodunit.

"Where you go, Madam?" the driver asked.

"Hemingway's, please."

"Madam, you want to go La Bodeguita del Medio?"

"Hemingway's."

"You mean, La Bodeguita," he tried to clarify, his poor diet a phlegmy slur in his throat.

"No, Hemingway's."

He raised his eyes, deciding that a mistake repeated three times becomes a fact and drove the taxi down the palm tree-lined driveway. The guardhouse lifted the barrier and they swung out onto the Malecón. Gwen imagined her husband sitting next to her frowning into his map, making sure that x marks the spot in his commonsensical mind.

The taxi swerved off the bustling promenade and away from the neon-lit hotels of Vedado. It accelerated past the fins of an aquatic-blue land shark and cruised along dark streets of a quiet gothic neighbourhood. Most of the ground level windows had been smashed and casually bandaged up with plywood, while clotheslines with shirts and blouses hung from window to window. Pavements were missing concrete nuggets and the entrances to antique buildings led to hollow shells containing only rubble from collapsed roofs. Gwen hated the past but liked history. She tried to imagine what the crumbling city must have looked like before its cornices deteriorated to dusty ruins.

They drove down an alleyway and came to a halt outside a building that looked like little more than a derelict stable. A squeezed group of locals gathered at the door, listening to the music blasting inside, careful not to bend the red fuchsia protruding from a flower box on the window ledge. The driver clicked on the Lada's interior light.

"Hemingway's, madam."

"You sure?" Gwen stepped out into the dark alleyway.

After checking the fare and tip, he replied, "La Bodeguita is Hemingway's, madam." Then he drove off in the only piece of machinery around, the sound of the diesel engine bleating against alley walls.

Gwen felt the men sizing her up in terms of meat and money. But she'd never in her adult life gone unnoticed in a public place and was well capable of dealing with leering men and jealous women. "Hello baby," one of them winked, a Caribbean smile acting as yin to the yang of his bald scarred head. Calmly she applied a layer of berry lip-gloss. Then dreading the inevitable pinch or rub reserved for single females, she squeezed by the locals, but they pressed themselves together to give her more space. A smiling corpulent bouncer chewed a cigar and waved her by.

The interior was what one would expect after viewing it externally. About fifty middle-aged tourists were squeezed into a space meant to accommodate twenty, some chanting "José! José!" at a guitarist. Graffiti covered the wall and even the ceiling. Gwen fanned her face with a beermat as people exhaled smoke on her as if she was a crop being dusted.

The counter was lined up with glasses of mint leaves ready to be transformed into mojitos. Gwen ordered one, threw it back and spied on the baseball-capped Canadians beside her. They were talking to a gorgeous young Cuban; they called him Elián. He wore Levi's and an open waistcoat framing a tanned chest. His deep brown eyes complemented his lustrous black hair and the lobe of his left ear was pierced with a shark tooth. Elián stared at Gwen and she felt her cheeks redden with the modest blush of coming first. At forty-seven she was still able to attract gorgeous young men.

In some ways Elián reminded Gwen of her husband, even though Paul was ten years her senior. When they'd originally met, Paul too had had an all-over tan, courtesy of his grandfather's peasant genesis in the Chalcidic peninsula of Macedonia. Originally she had been so enthralled to meet an older man with whom she'd had *everything* in common that she had surrendered to him completely. However, over the decades she had gradually realised that Paul was no Caesar but was just another centurion, his marriage trailing after him like a snail's slime.

Gwen threw back another mojito. She leaned on the counter and remembered back to when she was ten and finding it difficult to sleep because of the guilt of preferring a boy's love to God's. Life had been exceptional then.

She squeezed by Elián and tingled from the lingering peril of knowing exactly what he threatened to be. With her smile and eyes, she manipulated her way through the crowd. The stairs to the wash-room were narrow and she rubbed her palms along the cool plaster-work as she descended into what felt like a crypt.

The toilet was just a stained porcelain bowl with a chain and dim light bulb hanging from the ceiling. She looked around for a mirror. Suddenly the door swung open, shoving her forward, her face almost colliding with the wall.

Jacked up by fear, she spun about and snapped, "*I'm* in here."

Elián held up his hands.

With no one else around, Gwen was denied her trump card—making a scene. She glanced up. Her hand clutched the wooden handle of the toilet chain. She reckoned she could rip it free and plunge it through his eye socket.

"Shhhh, it's ok. If you scream, I in trouble." Elián spread his arms as if imploring his people not to crucify him. "*Big* trouble." He smothered her with presence, and his Adam's apple rose and fell beneath a fresh lawn of dark stubble. His breathing stuffed the room and then she realised that it wasn't his breathing filling her head but her own. His lips displayed his good-guy teeth and his demeanour said that for him life was a series of agreeable events. "I go now, Madam, or if you like . . ." He had the confidence of one who is never speechless because he knew that he was so good-looking that even when he strung together all the wrong words he'd still manage to come up with acceptable sentences. "I saw you on the top; no, that is wrong. *Upstairs* and boom! Big explosion in my heart." He clutched his chest and opened his waistcoat. His nipples were crowned with perfect brown aureoles and the left one was pierced with a silver ring. He gently took Gwen's hand and placed it over his pierced nipple. Aiming his smile at her, he seemed to flick through a grotesquerie of notions in his mind.

●

When she opened the door to leave, Gwen covered her face as the slant of luminosity burnt her eyes. She reached the top of the stairs and immediately exited the packed bar. It was one-thirty—she'd been gone an hour. That was the last thing she needed; a pacing husband in a white courtesy night-robe. Still, Gwen had the *fully-realised* confidence of an adventurer assured of a charmed existence, always convinced that not only would she conquer the latest intricate dilemma but of also emerging more formidable and prudent than before.

Settling into the sanctuary of a taxi, she tried to imagine having to tell Paul the truth. But how can a person know who they are if they give away their secrets?

In the elevator of the Hotel Nacional she stared at the gold-plated railings and wondered how many billion minute creatures, deposited by human after human, were layered in licentious infinitesimal orgies all over its shining surface. *God*, she thought, *I love life.*

Gwen slid the key card into the door. *Be in bed*, she thought, *be asleep.* The bedroom was bathed in the dim glow of the lamps she'd left on over an hour ago. Paul was under the blankets, breathing deeply. She imagined a train of 'Z's spewing from the pillow.

In the bathroom Gwen plucked a scented tissue protruding from a hole in the marble wall, as if from a magician's pocket. She craved a hot shower, but the water would make too much noise.

"Uh, honey?" A voice rose from a hoarse grunt to alarm. "Where are you?"

"Bathroom." Gwen cringed against her high-pitched forced-orthodoxy.

"I stayed awake for you," he mumbled, impatient to drop asleep again.

"Sorry." Roughly she scrubbed her hands before switching off the bedroom lamps. Gwen lowered the white skirt to the floor. Her side of the bed was warm and she sank into the heat of a recently departed body. Snuggling into her husband's back as if he was the epitome of the quixotic hero, she scratched her thigh and picked free a small glob of congealed semen. "Night-night, honey."

Melissa Diem

Electric Face

You with your lightning strike face fizzling in a roused-up fashion,
       sparking like space-mountain candy popping in my mouth,
you incite unbounded—striking lights along my spine
                         to the deliciously small glints in my mind,
     such a treacherous fusion gathers
                            as I trace and retrace every trace of you
         clipped to the neuron ready to ignite
                  at the thought   of electric face you.

The Day I Saw a Warrior Woman Fall

They came with their 2x4s,
impenetrable chests and papers that said
it all—just another trivial eviction.

They would have said, 'Sorry, ma'am,
it's not my problem,' if they lived in Orlando,
but they didn't.

One lived in a semi-d down the road
with a dog.
The guy in the middle had a kid

—just like hers!
So, they boarded up their faces instead
focused on the ground and a shoe shuffle,
                         (universal) ↑

while she screeched banshee-style
of every offence committed against every woman—
world-wide.

Hey—that's what you get when you hang out
with junkies—
they use you up.

She broke in the end, pleading
'Please, don't do this to me,'
and it brought me back

to two lost kids in Henry Street—
the three-year-old terrified
and blowing raspberries.

Renunciation of the World

If I had pigtails they would fly behind me
in preparation   for the renunciation of the world,
with a smile of course   I lay bubble wrap beds
3 meters thick   should the earth break on putting it down,
under the momentous weight of its dead   and more so the living.

Call it withdrawal or retreat—I am   daunted,
but then—when you're afraid of everything
it's a diminutive factor.   If I controlled all
I could have made *such a precedent*,   but I don't
and you're bigger than me so I lift small things   and always gently.

This is What Happened

The weather was serious,
the *Solanum Crispum Glasnevin* lifted
lost its grip in a squall—of such a command

it staked a day to retain to my mind—
the roof-flying type. Sidling caution up to the window,
I went with it—like a kid spinning in bluster,

keys, bag and sunglasses and I as lethal
flew in an over-shots delight, until the trees
of Newbridge, with a greater degree of contention

than me, threw sticks at the car and searing orange rods
flashed intermittently—three seconds in five—
'Beware' and 'Proceed with caution'

and it registered—I don't know
this alien planet atmosphere,
these trees, these people, these things.

A few provisions before a closed face
a formidable figure buds in my head,
cloak made of ravens sort of thing, and the usual—

pressure rising, thunderstorms imminent,
the sliding doors slid faster than normal.
Then a wind greater than me and willing to show me

a thing or two   blew me straight into you!
Though formidably dark and very visible,
I thought you as weightless as a hologram

I could slip through.

Loosening

Here is a thread, your head,
stick it in a bundle on your back,
the track is not apparent
until after it's been traced,

not held,
nor pinned,
nor shaped.

My head is loosening at the root,
I hear the grating grind
on top of the basal shoot,
raw dendrites weak and lax,

so eager to dismantle,
no longer willing to be bound
between the warp and weft
of this daily route.

As If

Face to face—the kitchen contents spilled out between us,
the heat of animal instinct flared its intentions   from the left
so unexpectedly,
                        we went for it—
                                    head on and colliding.
We were living it   like some sort of passion,
if we hadn't faltered   we might've gone all the way
as if we believed,
just for a moment,   as if we meant it.

The Angles of Your Hands

The angles of your hands
spanning wide and flying
conductors in a race,
tell me
you're explaining something.
Can you explain it to me?

Your hands disperse, rearrange
in patterns unexacting
in latitude,
but nonetheless
configured.

I know by you,
it's complex, unexpected,
something you can't quite
put your finger on
but will in time.

Your hands collapsed the day you spoke
of work commitment,
allotment of your time
and something about
my attitude.

Or was that altitude?

A Love Poem

I will give you carry way seeds
to sow within your worries. Stitch speckled sparrow wings

to fasten to your fear. Cut the threads
that hook your mind and set your angst on fire.

Peel back your skin and crush your bones,
teasing out the veins, twitching as we go.

Let me suck the breath from you and crack your tired skull
I will bring you far astray   to places scarcely dared—

Brenda Collins

The Breadcrumb Trail

(an excerpt)

Prologue

She hated spring: the devil you don't know. Winter was cold and raw, but at least it was predictable. With spring came the expectation of relief, of change, but it was a slow promise, realised fully only across several weeks. The sun was becoming adventurous, lingering a little later, but the air was still crisp and she still shivered at night when she tried to sleep on the dusty floor, back pressed to the wall of whatever skeletal building she was in on whatever night. Worse, her daughter was with her, who at just four years old knew nothing of heat and comfort, of sleeping on a full stomach, or of peace.

She watched her play with a small, plastic fire truck. One of the back wheels was missing and the white ladder on top had snapped near the base. She remembered the day she had found it, discarded on the street, and the strange shame that had followed just for the sheer delight it brought, as if every maternal effort she'd made up to that point had been an utter failure.

"Warm enough, sweetheart?" she asked, her breathing laboured. The cold air rattled in and out of her lungs and the cough that followed was as much a habit as it was ill-health. She dimly remembered biology classes from school years earlier, her teacher saying something about the thoracic diaphragm being one of the strongest muscles in the body and if you coughed hard enough for long enough, you could break a few of your own ribs. Running would be tricky with a broken rib. She tugged the thin jacket more tightly around herself.

The girl looked up at her mother for a second with wide blue eyes that were more iris than white, and then she nodded. It was always the same answer, whether the question pertained to hunger or happiness. She knew no other way. Yes, she supposed she was not hungry, but it was easy for her to say that when she had never really known what it meant to have enough.

She heard a distant burst of gunfire. A chain of familiar thoughts and questions—how many of them, how far away—ran the same weary path through her mind. Experience told her that they were too far away to signify a threat. Just the Border Patrol doing its routine circuit. They weren't likely to drift quite this far out; at least, not anytime soon. It was too early in the day to be that obvious. Still, her heart tightened a bit. They had become such a constant presence in her life that even when they weren't actually out looking for her, she had started to convince herself that they were. Time and repetition had burned into her head the image of their dark vehicles drifting down the streets, and driving them in patient hunt were the black-uniformed guards, their Kevlar helmets cutting a strange mush-roomed silhouette. She found herself expecting to see them around every corner, imagined the sound of them driving nearby and waited for shots that had not yet come her way. She was Pavlov's dog, conditioned to the point of exhaustion, and not sure how much longer she could keep going.

The night was quiet and hollow, the neighbourhood empty. Or, at least, empty on the surface. The streets there appeared deserted but the place came alive at night and she had sat watching enough times to know that there were actually plenty of people around— people like her: drifting on their own, with no sense of origin or destination. She tried to avoid them, even though they had virtually everything in common. They always seemed to emerge from the darkness and shuffle about in small numbers. Like her, they moved from place to place, going wherever the need took them, whether it was for shelter, food, or drugs. They were the faint pulse of an otherwise dead locality, a family to her one minute and aggressors the next, depending on the demands of their necessity. In truth, even after all her years of living exactly as they had, she still wasn't sure what to make of them. She would scrap with them for the same crumb of bread, but could not, in all honesty, blame them for what she lacked. If fingers were to be pointed, they would point North—north to the Border. To the Border Patrol. To the Government. To the enclosed City and all its inhabitants, sated and comfortable, who spoke the same language, had once received broadly the same education, lived under the same flag, but had more money and could afford the price tag of their rights.

Her stomach rumbled and for a moment she almost couldn't hear the rolling cracks of gunfire. The commotion didn't sound any nearer or farther away. *The Dead Zone*, she thought. The Dead Zone was any place that was situated right beside the Border. It was a hotspot of Insurgent-Patrol conflict and the Insurgents always came out the ass-end of it. They were an Outsider militia who protested against the Government's policies, especially the existence of the Border. It was a largely fruitless means of demonstration for them: the Patrol had resources at its disposal; Insurgents had leftovers. They played the boy-shepherd of the David and Goliath story but without the underdog ending. Insider media pounced on the fighting and since the newspapers and stations were politically owned, Insurgents were painted as the zealots, while the Patrol were the toughened heroes. All in all, it was easy for Insiders to rationalize everything that went on at the Border and beyond it. Blacklisting and rumours of questionable interrogation techniques never made it to the front page and neither did this cat-and-mouse game they played with her. They weren't even supposed to venture away from the Border into Outsider territory, but they did—regularly. Neighbouring Outsider districts quickly became regular loops of their patrols. There had been some rumblings initially from their superiors and the last of the journalists, but it had died down fairly quickly. It was easy for the Patrol to defend its actions. The excuses were obvious: they were pre-empting Insurgent conflict. Some people thought 'provoked' was a more accurate term, but it depended on which side of The Border you lived, naturally.

She stopped, listening to sounds in the hall outside—the slurred mutterings of drunks. *Time to think about moving.* The Patrol was looking for her but it was tricky finding anyone outside of the City now. There were no databases to locate people. Registered addresses weren't worth a damn any more. If you wanted to find someone Outside, you had to know somebody else and the Patrol weren't known for having that rapport. They had a reputation for using fists and instruments where words failed them—so when they picked up locals and questioned them, often even a hint of this threat proved effective. In her case, how fruitful their yield of information depended on how many people knew her. To counter this, she moved on to another building or another part of town once a week, never getting comfortable or familiar, never knowing anyone. Her stomach growled again, a little painfully this time. Sitting on the floor in the empty cold of spring, she listened with a sense of fragile comfort to her daughter's contented hums as she played with her broken toy.

Chapter 1

Jane

It was Trader's Day and there was that electricity in the air. It was the buzz of possibility, even if it never translated into anything. Thousands of people milled slowly around in their obscure, improvised fashions, weaving between clusters of tables, boxes and crates. The clutter of ware was displayed in a shabby imitation of the psychology that shops and legitimate businesses had once employed. People advertised their trade on anything they could find: damp card, blackboards, whiteboards, bits of wood, or the blank reverse of bank statements that littered the streets near the City. The market district was spread out over a vast area, stretching easily into empty, unpopulated land to meet the needs of both sellers and customers. The range of goods up for trade was impressive considering it had been cobbled together from a destitute community. Food, guns, alcohol, drugs, electronics, art, books, music. It was all in there somewhere—depending on supply, demand and the political mood. The terms of trade were unregulated and changeable, and had the makings of remarkable interaction. People sometimes came just to watch because often they had nothing else. Jane Kennedy pressed herself up on to her toes and strained to see over the small crowd of people who had gathered around. People shifted in and out of the phalanx and she craned her head left and right to peer between limbs, catching glimpses of the exchange beyond. The conversation was muffled behind the wall of bodies and their murmured commentary, but they grew silent with interest. She squeezed between two tall men and found a cozy vantage-point for herself, smiling at the comfort of gathering body heat.

"Where'd you get it?" the buyer asked.

"Fell off the back of a truck."

The group thrummed with a collective chuckle when they heard this.

"And the dog ate my homework," someone added.

Even the seller laughed along. If things really fell out of trucks as often as that story was used, they would have to wade through a sea of free merchandise just to get to the Trade. And considering the number of people who made the trip every week, many of them doing no more than ruefully watching others buy and sell while they simply hoped for the best, it was obvious that there weren't that many careless hauliers around. The buyer set something wrapped in a cloth on the table, as well as money bundled together with an elastic band. The seller nodded to another man standing behind who was noticeably armed. He stepped forward and opened the cloth, picking up a 9mm pistol. He murmured the model to the seller as he examined the weapon. They watched him as he loaded and unloaded the empty magazine, cocked the hammer, tested the safety, squeezed a few empty rounds. For a minute, all the attention was focused on him and the delicate clicking and snapping of his inspection. He nodded his approval after another few seconds. The seller picked up the cash and laid it out. The currency was a mixture of yen, euro, rubles, and a variety of dollars. The seller slowly, calmly counted through and calculated its total value in one currency.

"Add a hundred," he murmured.

"Fifty," the buyer said, a little indignantly.

"Eighty-five."

"Seventy. That's as high as I can go."

The seller mulled it over, playing his part as the hard-pressed dealer, then nodded. They stared as the buyer removed another selection of bills from his inner pocket and counted out the difference. Jane watched with intrigue. Money had a cameo role at The Trade. There wasn't much of it floating around outside of the City and it was generally kept for things that could not be bartered for within the market. She watched the seller sort through it and check its authenticity. Once he was satisfied, they shook hands. The laptop was packed into its Styrofoam frame and cardboard box and the buyer clutched it to him, walking away swiftly. The crowd dispersed slowly and they talked it through amongst themselves, dissecting the details of the trade. Bad deal. Jane shook her head and turned towards a table behind her that was laden with containers of books. The seller was sitting in a rusty collapsible deck-chair, bundled up in layers and a parka against the cold February evening. Between the hat that was pulled down to his eyebrows and the scarf that was wrapped up to his mouth she could see hardly any of his face. He nodded to her in acknowledgment and pulled the scarf down for a second to sip something steaming from the Thermos mug clutched between his gloved hands.

"It's a cold one," he said. Jane nodded. Having spent the last few hours walking around and unloading buckets of seasonal fruit and vegetables, she didn't feel it as much. She looked down into a crate of books, scanning over the titles of the ones near the bottom. She leaned over and reached in with both hands, moving them aside.

"Looking for something specific?"

She glanced at him.

"Maybe. I thought…"

There. She leaned in a little more and pulled out a large volume, easily a thousand pages. It was a medical manual, dog-eared and yellowed from sunlight. She flicked through it, scanning over subsections.

"Always handy to have one of those," he said.

"Yes," Jane murmured vaguely.

"Interested?" he asked.

She gave a shrug. "Yeah..."

She read more carefully through a part near the end, then flipped back to the imprint page.

"How much?"

"Ordinarily I'd say… fifty. But for you, forty."

Jane exhaled a quiet chuckle.

"Too steep for what I'd be getting, I'm afraid."

She snapped the book shut.

"What exactly did you have in mind?"

"Well, let's see. It's not in the best condition and it's over fifteen years old, so there have probably been seven or eight newer editions since. The section on medication is the most valuable and it's not up-to-date. So I'm thinking… twenty."

The hat moved on his brow as he widened his eyes. He shook his head.

"Sorry. Can't feed myself on losses. I paid good money for that book."

"Is that why there's a library stamp on it?"

He was silent.

"Look," she continued. "The original RRP is only slightly more than what you're selling it for now and that was almost twenty years ago. Thirty is the best I can do."

"You're killing me," he said, grinning.

She shrugged. "Pretty sure I can locate a more recent edition for the same or less in the next couple of weeks. You *know* you're getting a good deal here."

He made a show of thinking it over, muttering to himself an improvised pity-me calculation of the numbers. Jane glanced at her watch and waited, deadpan.

"I can't resist a pretty face," he said finally. Jane gave him a smile of scepticism and handed over the money. He held the bills up to the thinning sunlight and thumbed them carefully.

"Enjoy," he said and stuffed the bills into a pocket inside his parka. Jane put the book in a canvas bag and moved off.

"Maybe I'll see you at the next Trade..." he called after her. Jane had to smile.

"Yeah, maybe."

She strode quickly past the tables and makeshift stalls. She could smell the warm juices of food as she drifted past the food sellers. Her stomach groaned longingly after the scent of cooked meat and she thought briefly back to her childhood and teen years, when meat had been an assumed regular of her mother's culinary repertoire. If she and her friends had it once a fortnight now it was as much. Realising she was running late, she picked up her pace and made her way toward a field of hundreds of parked cars, many of them dirty, dented and scratched. She spotted Ray and waved to him.

"Hey."

"You're on your own," Jane said, smiling brightly. "Does that mean I'm not the late one this time?"

He shook his head. "They're waiting in the car. Said they didn't want to stand in the cold again while you figured out the difference between the big hand and the small hand."

"Sorry," she said. "I was watching a show."

"Did you get anything?"

"Medical manual." She reached into her bag and pulled it out. "It's dated, but there's still some relevant information and it covers the fundamentals in good detail. I couldn't resist."

Ray nodded mild approval before distractedly pushing his fingers through his unkempt blond hair. Thirty years old and he was still too lazy to trade something for a comb. Or just borrow someone else's.

"Did the others get anything?"

He shrugged. "Jason got six jars of peanut butter."

"And you managed to trade the stuff we brought?"

Ray yawned as they turned back to their own vehicle. "Yeah. It all went and we got food and fuel for it."

"Good. I'm starving. Some people were just sitting there freezing their asses off. Couldn't sell a thing."

"I know," he murmured. "Thank God for the farm."

Ray's parents lived on a farm. A lot of the land was idle, but they'd always kept a large patch of ten acres or so for their own needs and it was treasured at times like this, when global structures had crumbled and trade had shrunk to the local level. His father had died of the flu years before and his mother wasn't able to keep it all going herself. Food was one of the most valuable things around now and the opportunity to work the farm often meant they went to sleep at night with something in their stomachs. What they didn't use themselves was traded for other foodstuffs, fuel, medicines and toiletries. Or to improve neighbourly relations, which was often just as valuable.

"Did you catch any interesting trades?" he asked.

"Well, overall it was a very sensible day. Just the small things, you know? But I saw a new laptop pass hands just before I came here. That's why I was late."

He looked at her. "They're not around every day. And even when they are, they're hard to shift. Did it sell?"

"Not cheaply."

"What did he trade for it?"

"Practically his soul," Jane laughed quietly to herself as details of the man's somewhat desperate proffers flashed into her head. The market hum faded as they ascended a small grassy hill. She caught sight of a small group of people gathered around one vehicle. One or two of them waved and as they got closer Jane saw that Ava was clutching several tubes of toothpaste and floss in her hands. If you lived outside the City where health services were barely functioning, everyone took care of themselves and oral hygiene was a high priority for a lot of people. Many would rather suffer a bullet than a toothache. Ava was in a class of her own though. She lived in mortal fear of cavities and did everything in her power to prevent the mere possibility from arising. Jane pulled a bunch of keys from her pocket, casting a look at Jason as he dug a finger deep into a jar of peanut butter and stuck a lump of it into his mouth. Jane held the keys out to Ray.

"Can you drive back? I want have a look through that book."

He took the keys.

Máirín O'Grady

Bereavement

Mammy Crying Forever in Heaven and Daddy Moaning on the Floor.
Auctioneers heaving him out the door kicking cans in front of them.
>They're making piles outside in the garden with the furniture.
>And myself and the sister
>with small sticks debating to resist them. The Farm's covered
in whiskey and daddy sprinkling it over the corn. The cattle leering
crooked in the fields and the sheep belching to be shorn.
>The House and Farm for auction
>and twelve decades of Treacy's Run Out Of Dunmore.
Mammy's eyes telling us she'll have to leave us.
Half way out the avenue Hair turned Grey with Fear I'll have to
>Leave ye now
>babies. And my sister dragging over a bucket and a mop
for the Tears. and I'm saying mammy mammy don't go leaving us now
mammy don't go breaking My Heart Now Mammy. Holding Teddy
Bears. I See Every Line On Her Face.
>To this day I can see every single line on her face.
I can see how the Hair grows in her Ears. I'm saying mammy don't
you go leaving us now. Rising from
a broken bed in the avenue mammy's saying I'm leaving ye now
Angels.

Rubbing our hair on the arm chairs in the garden ejected from
the farm. The Kitchen Table set up outside on the lawn Pint Glasses
and sandwiches and the lampshades lit at dawn.
Daddy Bawling at a Storm and Mammy's Face in the Sky.

                    My black eyed sister with the mop
                    soaking tears from my eyes. Dragging
the bucket for the dogs to have a drink and a bucket to wash the cat
and the neighbours Gawking at the Gate Post reach up to tip their Hats.

            My sister mopping the liquid from our hearts running
down the avenue.

           And myself holding
           the armchair for something to hold on to.
The donkey's in bad form and daddy feeding him a bottle of Jameson.
And mammy heading out the avenue
saying; promise me ye'll look after your daddy When I'm Gone.

        Wheel your daddy to the Hospital if your daddy feels sick.
And hold your daddy's hands when ye're Guiding him Home from
                        Cummins'.
And collect your daddy in the Hearse when ye're driving him home
                      from Funerals.
  My sister bringing the bucket for the tears
  to cook daddy's cabbage in.
And mammy calling after her not to forget to Look after Him.

        From the gate mammy's calling he's the best man in Ireland.
        He'd take the shirt off his back for you.
        He'd Light Himself on Fire for You.
My father bare backed climbing up the hill with a box of matches. Looks
out over the Farm.
And hangs a sign in the Trees.
"Michael Treacy's Dead."

Ties

Now mammy are you alright there are you right? Now strap your-self in there now. Oh oh hands. Ha hands. These. These. You're alright there now mammy aren't you? Now you're alright. Now you're buckled tight ha? You love driving mammy? Ma ma I. It's warmer in here now isn't it? Back in the car. You'll be back in the home in no time. Ugh. Bogged in. Changing gear. Well the evenings are getting longer now ha? There's a better stretch in them now ha? Rain belts either side. Yes there is now mammy what? We're getting in to April now sure. Lord. Our. Our. Trees tunnel and shake. Will you have a sweet now mammy? Here I've opened it here for you just to put it into your mouth. Gum gums and teeth. Now isn't that lovely now ha? In teeth ugh. Do you remember mammy? You used to bring us bullseyes in the back of Jim's car when we'd go to visit daddy in Carlow? Jim'd be watching his seats ha? Rain belting either side. To keep us quiet when we'd have to go into daddy. Sheep drenched through the trees. To keep us from crying ha? To keep him from crying. Eyes eyes. Face in his strapped hands can you bring me home? I feel better now? I really feel better. Like rain I am right. Stuck toff toffee. Matt was saying he'd try and be out to you shortly now mammy ha? Car rattling. I'd say you miss Matt now what? Warm warm straps. Brown water rests in troughs. Sides of the road. Well he's busy at the taxis ha? He's driving all day every-day now. Stuck in huh. Driving the wheels off the car ha? Oh yeah. Ughhuh fingers. Fingers stuck. Oh yeah now. Isn't that right ha? Uh. Belt. Belt around arms. And he's spraying the corn now in there. With the few fine days he gets. Crows fly away from windows. And Eddie's Andy's cutting it again now for him this harvest. Two. Both boys and sheers. Green grass shears in hands glint of steel. Ugh ughhuh belt tight. Remember now when it'd be Matt and Eddie cutting it and you'd sing here comes two fine lads cutting down the corn. Here comes as fine a two sons as ever a woman bore. Ha? Crows. Uhh. You'd feel the stretch in the evenings now mammy? You'd feel the stretch alright ha? Uh and strapped. And Matt's going to let the cattle out any day now mammy ha? He's going to let them out into Eddie's fields. The day. Fire coming out the windows of the house. Mattie with a line of chalk. Eddie shots in the air. Shotgun strap across his arm. So they'll be closer to Matt now than renting off of Learys now that Eddie's gone to stop the arging. Ha? Trembling rosary beads round the rearview. Stuck. Sure next Sunday if they're out we can drive past and see them out the window? You'd like to see them. The steam rises on the back window and the steam on the windscreen. It's lovely now in spring when they're let out. They lose it altogether trapped inside for the full winter. Ugh huh. Stuck in a shed for months they only see light when Mattie opens the door to feed them. Huh trap. The little breeds get confused in the dark says Matt. Oh uh. Their little feet get hurt on the slats. Uh uh. They lose their sense in the dark. Stuck. Straps on hands ohh. Oh uh uh ohhh. Tied. Tied. Oh mammy don't be crying. We're nearly there. We'll be back now in the home in no time. Oh ho oho. Please don't cry mammy. Look we're nearly there now. Oho ho. This is killing me. It's killing me. I'll play the song mammy I'll play the song. I'll put on the tape. I'll put on the tape. Oh noho. Oh uh ho. Don't cry mammy don't cry now. You remember me? You remember me? It's Bernie. The tape's starting. Mammy? Mammy mammy it's Bernie. Soft voices softly singing silent night holy night all is calm all is bright round yon virgin mother and child.

Mice

A frosty, foggy night. A black van parked on stage facing out to the audience. Two old men walk towards it. A door slams in the distance from the house they have left, and an outside light is switched off leaving them in darkness. Man B walks stiffly to the driver's side turning on the headlights. Man A limps with pronounced difficulty past the headlights into the passenger side. Man B nervously fiddles with the headlights and the window wipers, starting the van. Man A in non-verbal emotional distress. The car radio going in and out of signal as the men drive, transmitting white noise and muddled voices throughout.

B: Cold cold day and a cold cold night. Frost'd kill you. Cleave you in two. You could be found dead. Found dead in the middle a the road. White frost covering ye. *(Pause)* The dogs freezing. Dogs freezing in their beds. One eye open to the sky.

A woman's voice breaks through white noise of the radio

VOICE: Oh Mammy left without a fire. Falling in dirt going out for a sod.

Voice lost again in white noise. A remains in silent distress. Vigourously rubbing his brow and jaw with his hands.

B: Finished journeying. Finished journeying. No more miles. No more miles for us now after that. Feet only. Feet only and inches. Too far and further.

VOICE: Mammy waiting in black days and nights for someone to come or go.

B: Too far and further. Home now. Home again. Glensmullach Glensmullach in the quiet crossroads. Nyther god nor man near us. Donkey donkey in the stable does be lonely. Straw up round his feet. Moths in the field is company.

VOICE: Misery in a damp bed. The misery of Mammy. The whispers I've endured this day.

B: Dogs'll be crying crying froze above. Trying to get near a bit of rug for warmth. Mind the dogs. Mind them dogs. *(Pause)* Morning now everything white. Frost stuck along the roads. Trees and hedges covered. Sheep in the fields crying for a bite of grass. *(Pause)* Glensmullach at the cross roads. Born and reared and rarely left. Us us now in the dark. No candle now. No flame in the window. *(Pause)* Quiet again. Mice froze in their holes. *(Pause)* We'd need light now. Bit a light going down the avenue. Dark avenue. Dark avenue. A flashlight flashlight now to mind them potholes. You'd kill yourself now in them potholes.

VOICE: Mammy with the bread blue in the press and Johnny feeding pheasants to dogs. Oh the whispers in my ears today.

A becoming more and more distressed at the voice.

B: You could fall into one. Fall in fall in fall in and you'd never be got out of it. Never be got out of it at all. Down a hole and nyther god nor man. Only the birds in the dark seeing your hat your hat left lying on the lane. *(Pause)* Have we a flashlamp flashlamp there to see with? *(B switches on the light inside the van and looks around in the back for a torch. With the rear of the van now illuminated dead pheasants can be seen hanging from the ceiling.)* Might be ashes left might be a few ashes yet now when we're back. Glensmullach. Glensmullach at a quiet crossroads. Nyther god nor man. Neether god nor man. Nyther near us at all. *(Pause)* Us us and the birds. No mammy. No candle. No flame in the window.

VOICE: Youse fools. Dragging mammy out behind a shed for the toilet with a flash lamp at night. The women like a hive a wasps around the graveside whispering. Two clowns a hell. Ye couldn't keep a rat in a biscuit tin. Oh my mother froze in the kitchen with that speechless eejit. And Johnny the bigger fool with a cap on taking charge a minding mice at the crossroads. Drive home away from here now and when yez close close the door tonight ye may seal it behind ye.

White noise takes over again

A: *(Weeping)* She were very very cross.

B: The two of us now. Two of us two of us. Either either side of the small fire small fire. Nyther god nor man. Two pair two pair the two of us two of us. We'll crawl in the door now crawl in crawl in. The dogs won't even open an eye. We'll be dead now dead quiet an we heading in. Quiet quiet quiet now as mice. Down down along the avenue. Neether god nor man. Nyther god nor man. Just ourselves ourselves now. Us and the birds. Us us and the birds in the dark.

Grief

I bought him for my first communion and his name was sandy. He hid under the table in naas but I dragged him out and bought him because i loved him. I cut all my dolls' hair weird and had no one and everything became sandy. We played detectives together. The cats weren't happy and we killed them all by putting poison in their food. Well daddy killed them all by putting poison in their food. We named him sandy. Daddy killed all the cats and so we wouldn't see them he went around at night looking for dead cats and picked them up where he could see them. He threw them all in sack. A cat sack for dead cats. And then burnt the sack full of dead cats in the dump down the yard. Sandy knew and didn't say anything. Even though we were both detectives he never said. Ratty sandy. He had yellow eyes and looked at me from the ground but i couldn't warm to him after that. So he became my mother's dog. And followed her around. To the washing line. He won her two goldfish once at a school field day where daddy drove the children around on a trailor in circles and circles screaming. But sandy won mammy two fish dancing a hornpipe. We named the fish patricia and liam. They had two hundred children in our pond and one day i saw patricia in the pond and she had a huge tumour on her side and had grown to the size of a mackerel. If i stabbed her with a pitchfork would her blood be red. I hated patricia. Sandy became fat. And couldn't go on walks when mammy walked for five miles a day to go from a size eighteen to a size twelve to fourteen. I preferred her bigger but daddy mustn't have. Sandy bit me on the face one day when i tried to pick him up to move him when he lay down like a tree in front of my auntie's car. My auntie said not to blame him that sandy didn't mean it. But it was my face. And i felt that a bite on the face was stretching it. I couldn't fully forgive sandy and watched his yellow eyes on the ground. One day a man who lived in a caravan in our back garden drove in the avenue flying and ran over sandy's back and i'd been asking for a ferret a ferret please. But i heard sandy shriek from the playroom and they've got me a parrot! They've got me a parrot! But i went outside and it was sandy with his spine all twisted. I ran to the pond and screamed at hideous patricia swimming around. Sandy lived but also lost his ability to have sandies with other dogs. The vet said that. Sandy got fatter and lived to be fifteen. When mammy died sandy walked inside past all the crowds standing in the hall where the coffin was in the sittingroom on a sunny day with all the doors and windows open and flowers everywhere like it was a communion or a confirmation. And sandy lay down under the coffin with my mother lying over him with her hands folded and her eyes closed and her mouth twisted and in this suit that was for winter and it was summer but we liked the suit and it would keep her warm. Everyone thought sandy was marvellous. They'd never seen a dog do that in their natural lives. That's loyalty for you now. You see they'd know pets. But I think sandy knew there was a party and thought that there might be food. After we'd buried my mother and came back to the house sandy got too much food off all the people and couldn't go to the toilet properly for a week. I saw him from the windows hunched over in the field but he couldn't get it all out. And he wanted attention at the party but he smelt weird because he was old now and no matter how loyal he had been no one wanted to rub him at all. Sandy grew a huge tumour on the side of his mouth and we had it removed. And the first vet's daughter who had now taken over because her father had premature alzheimers and wandered around the roads if he managed to unlock the door said that sandy should now be ok again after his tumour was removed. But it grew back again twice as bad. And he disgusted me like patricia and he couldn't get up properly off the floor and he went deaf and all he wanted was food. So we went back to the vet and she said it had progressed and his lungs were filled with tumours and his ears and he had almost no interior left he was so filled with tumours. And sandy bit vets all the time so we had to sedate him before she injected him with this huge needle full of raspberry flavoured liquid that's actually blue that was going to stop his heart. And he had to have his paw shaved. So while we were waiting for the sedative to kick in i asked the vet what happens to sandy's body and she said we should bring him home to bury him. But daddy didn't want to dig a hole in the cold or bring a dead dog home for fifteen minutes in the car so we asked her could she dispose of him and she said that there was a man who took away all the bodies of dogs but charged forty euro to which we agreed and that he burnt all the bodies and you could get your dog's ashes back but that cost an extra twenty so we let that part be. And the vet injected sandy with raspberry flavoured liquid that's actually blue and his heart stopped straight away. She kept touching his eyes to see if he was dead because that's the last reflex to go. And he was but he kept twitching for ages afterwards and wet the floor. She said no no he is dead even a piece of meat cut from a carcass will keep twitching for up to half an hour because cells in the muscles still have energy. And we drove home in the car and closed the door behind us.

Happiness

Sit on the sand banks sit on the Hills. lie in the Bog with your Feet in a
Bog Hole of a fine day. of a Fine Day in May.
          Sit under a furze bush
                    when you've fallen
               off your Horse. and change
          your face change your face on your way to school in a
garage behind the neighbour's house. Mind the ponies drinking from
               the canals. sliding Feet in Reeds
          sliding in. The horses
galloping trying to catch the train. On a Fine
          Day. Oh Your Fine May Days. Watch
     from the bridge the workmen in red cars from the bypass to their
     bungalow's. Lit sittingrooms and children on their knees. Daddy
                    Daddy your knees! On a fine day.
          Of fine days in may. There's a child talking
to a dog on a turfbank behind a red shed. There's a dog talking
to a child in the Grass in the Middle of the Road. There's crows
          on the rungs of a car trailer fly
               ing through the trees. Watch an army
     of cattle watch another army of cattle across the barbed wire that
          divides their fields. and Lie Down in a Field of Thistles.

Oh we've
all Kinds of Weeds! You
wouldn't believe the weeds
we have. We've
Weeds the Height of Trees. Weave Weeds
into Hairbands for your cousins. On a fine day.
Oh your fine fine
days. find a badgers tongue on the train tracks.
find Shea Hayes asleep in a citroen at the foot of the bridge.
Watch Shea Hayes in a citroen drift
across the main road.
and bring Michael for a Cycle. Yourself and Michael on the Bi
cycle. Close the door
and put out the dog and tell them
your Mother's Gone to the Bog on a
fine day in May. Of a fine fine day. Put Cherry
Blossoms in your Ham Sandwich and eat them under the
hawthorne tree. And see Pat mowing over glass in his avenue.
Put your money
on the derby winner.
it's Willie Wynn. Will He Win? Or Won't He? Thunder
down on the Curragh. Thunder falling
on the Curragh. rain lashing up dust. count the Dust on your Arms in
the Trees. Two
ninety
nines
and a child's cone with a flake. Flake
the Day off into your Icecream. Keep your Nanny in the house before
she dies of heat. on a great day for drying. a great day for drying when
it's a fine day. On a fine day
in May. This is
the Width of the World. The Width of the Earth is Three Fine
Miles. The Pink White Blue of hydrangeas
over lime content inside
countryside soil. There's a tree

in the lake. There's birds on the branch of the
tree. There's birds on the branch of the tree of the tree in the lake. Roll
in the water till your saddle breaks. And running
free. Running Free like an elephant
with the Birds
on the Beach on a fine day. of a fine day in May.
Mammy won two fish Dancing a Jig in the field day. we kept the dog
on the lead to stop him dancing.
lie down in a Field of Hay under
Planes Roaring. Tonight
you're the white pony beside the Castle on the River. Sing
to your Horse over Fences. Sing to your horse like the Bird in the
Hedges. And sneeze the Day
out of your mind. and look at the Day on the tissue
in front of you. On fine days. Of fine days when
We Had Them. Days On The
Plate
in Front of You. On a Blue swing swinging in Yellow
trees. Of a
fine day. Of all them fine days of May.

Martin Malone

Ritual

I spread the newspaper on the kitchen table, knowing for certain that he will be there to stare at me with his murderer's eyes, as he is each anniversary of Alex's death. Every year the newspapers pick up on the quadruple killer and for the last few years there is increasing speculation in the media about his release from prison.

My pink Nokia does a little jig on the wooden surface between the red and white salt and pepper cellars. I pick it up and see Nano's number in the caller display.

"Vicky," she says.

"I know. I'm looking at the bastard."

Silence.

Nano says, "I'll call round later, okay?"

"Okay."

I need to think, to clear my head, to prepare for the annual ritual, the cleansing...

•

Two days after our first big row over money, Alex came home and told me that he'd volunteered for the Leb. I went crazy because I wanted him to be around when our baby was born. But then he said he'd only put his name forward to push himself farther up the list for the next trip. It made sense to me when he said it like that and when I calmed down I realised that he was right; we needed the money. I said I wouldn't mind if he went after our baby was born. I often wondered if he'd pushed that news at me to break part of the storm. That he knew he was going all along.

We hadn't got married quarters yet because I wouldn't take the one the quartermaster wanted to issue us; it was some dive, the walls rank with damp and peeling wallpaper. There was an outdoor toilet with the shit backed up in it and of course Alex wanted the kip as he didn't want to pay rent for the flat. And even though the rent for the quarters cost next to nothing, I refused to move in there. People bank on other people being desperate enough to accept anything that's thrown at them and, what's more, to be grateful for it.

"Ah, Vicky," he said.

"Ah, Vicky my arse. Jesus, get me out of here. If my ma saw the state of the gaff you wanted to move me into, she'd be after yer blood, Alex."

"I'll get it cleaned up."

"Why bother cleaning something that should have been knocked down a hundred years ago?"

So Alex started talking about buying our own place. He said they were building a rake of new houses out in Tallaght, and he kept this up for a couple of weeks and then he said, when he'd brought home a takeaway from the Chinese restaurant, that he had some news. I'd known he was building up to something but hadn't been too sure what it was. His oul one was always full of mad schemes: like wanting us to buy a mobile home and park it in her backyard.

"I will in my hole," I'd said to Alex at the time.

If he couldn't see why not, then there was no sense in telling him. I wouldn't be under a compliment to anyone who would go and tell the world.

I was watching *Top of the Pops* on the telly and he thought I was just going to fall over him. When he was watching *Match of the Day* he didn't let on to me asking him to get me a bar of Aero; starving for it, I was. Anyhow, I loved that song *Fame* and, even with the small rise in me I could dance as well as what's her name.

When I was ready, I said—saying it like I didn't really care whether he told me or not—"What's your news, Alex?"

I was half-thinking he'd tell me he'd been selected for a potential NCO's course and would be away training a lot of the time, in the Glen of Imaal and that; I would hardly see him for six months.

"It'll wait," he said.

I'd hoped he wasn't getting the sulks.

"Tell us, how was your day?" he asked.

It was a cold summer evening and the fire was on one bar to save the gas in the bottle and I was carrying a cruel headache. I was still working in Dunnes and would be for as long as I could manage to stick it, til the baby came.

I told him my feet were sore and I'd had a massive row with a customer who said I'd overcharged her when I knew for a fact that I hadn't, because I'd triple checked her change seeing as it was her.

"What do you mean?" she'd said.

"Sure you're in here every week trying that oul trick on."

And she had been and the supervisor knew it too, but he said afterwards that I couldn't speak to the customers like that—because even though you were right, he said, the wrong way of accusing someone can be turned and used against you. I was just being straight is all. That one would lick shite if she thought it'd fill her.

Alex laughed at that.

He was wearing his combat uniform. I knew he wasn't supposed to be wearing it outside of barracks and had been warned about it by the military police a couple of times. He could wear his ordinary everyday uniform. I think it was to do with the combat jackets—the lads sold them or they were stolen. A security thing, I suppose, with the stuff that was going on up north. The combats were green and had good and plenty of pockets and the lads on the building sites were mad for them.

He sat in close beside me, lounged, and touched my belly with his fingertips and then laid his hand flat on it and kissed my cheek and didn't even take his hand away when I said I had a splitting headache, which told me he wasn't after anything.

"The CO brought me into the office today," he said.

I smelt drink off him, but it wasn't very strong; he'd only supped enough to give himself courage.

"For what?" I said.

Alex had lovely green eyes and they were full of life and maybe it was the alcohol had got behind them and polished them up, for they really shone that evening.

"He said I was selected for overseas."

I sat up straight, my spine going rigid, like lightning hitting a rod, and snapped, "No way, Alex!"

I was on my feet, evading his reach for me, and was at the table before he had even stood. That pitiful look he sometimes put on made my blood boil. I reached for the takeaway and I was that vexed I threw it at him and spattered his combats with rice and chicken curry.

"Vicky, for fuck's sake."

"You lied to me, Alex!"

When Alex got excited, he joined up his words and stood on his toes a little. It was like the words would kill him if he allowed them stay inside for any length. He put his hands out to beg for peace. I saw that stupid silver Claddagh ring his stupid mother had bought him the Christmas before, buying it for him after me telling her it was what I was getting him for a present. Such a cow, and me having to leave it in the shop where I was paying off it and instead buy him a silver chain and cross which he lost after a week. He put a foot forward.

"Fuck off! Don't you come near me, Alex."

He backed away and began smoothing his cropped brown hair. *Come on Eileen* came on the telly and we liked to dance to that and it was awkward listening to it because all I wanted to do then in that moment was dance with him. But he couldn't see this, he missed that, and if he had stepped forward, I wouldn't have stopped him coming the full journey. He didn't see it because he was gone and I was left alone with an upset baby in me and the strains of a happy pop song bouncing off the walls in a flat that smelt of curry.

•

He was always sending me home parcels from the Leb, full of baby clothes, pink and blue, and he'd said the stuff was really cheap out there and he'd the neck to be sending me crotchless knickers for when I'm better; meaning for when I'd be able to do the sex again.

I missed him more than I thought I would. It wasn't till he left that I realised the little things that he did around the place. Cleaning out the ashes, putting out the dustbin, washing the delph, listening and not talking, just being a pair of ears for me for whenever I had a row with Mammy or I was low in myself. I missed the warmth of him in the bed and the heat he would leave behind when he was just out of it, the way it was there for me to slide over on to, and I always slept better in the ghost of his heat. Funny that.

He wrote a lot of letters and this was hard for him because he'd left school when he'd turned thirteen, taken out of it by his ma to go work on a fuel lorry. His ma's a bollocks, were Nano's first words of friendship to me. I cracked up laughing because I'd never heard a woman being called that before.

Short letters and usually saying the same thing over and over, and he couldn't spell. His reading wasn't great, either. I'd have to read him the good bits out of the porn mags we liked to read in bed. I preferred the mags to the blue films; sometimes these were okay to watch but more often were not. I wouldn't be prudish or anything but that's how I am, I prefer sex and that in the mags to watching the vids that Alex sent home—I gave them to the girls to watch and they thought they were fucking brilliant, especially the one with the man who had a huge cock.

The girls could be a scream and I missed going out with them, but I was too big and I wasn't in the mood for them after about an hour in their company. They'd get too loud and when they got like that I went distant in myself for I couldn't see the sense of what the loud laughter was all about. I did before, but maybe being with a baby changes you.

•

"That's fucking lovely," Nano'd said, trying on the gold rope chain Alex had sent me for my 24th birthday.

We were in my flat the evening before the world caved in.

"Yeah, it's lovely alright."

"He's got good taste, Vicky, I'll say that for him."

"He has, hasn't he?"

"My Gerry's taste is in his hole."

"Ah, he's not that bad."

"He fucking well is."

Then I remembered that he'd surprised her with a cake and a band singing *you're once, twice and three times a lady* in the mess and she was mortified because this was the song that was playing when she and Mouldy Jones were having sex during one of the nights Gerry was on duty and he got stuck in her and couldn't get out and we had to call an ambulance. None of us knew till that night that a man could literally be trapped inside you. Gerry never found out and if he did he couldn't very well say anything because he used to go with Maggie Doyle and no man who had respect for his mickey would go near her. Walking, she is.

"You're right about Gerry's taste," I said.

"In his hole."

"Tea?"

"I'll make it. You've the place looking lovely. Who painted it up for you?"

"Michael."

"The same Michael you used to go with?"

"That was ages ago."

"He's good, isn't he?" she'd said, looking around.

"He is."

"Did he charge much?"

"He wouldn't take anything."

"That was decent of him."

"He said I was to tell no one. In case anyone else would expect it done for free."

"You told me."

"You're not no one."

And she reached over and put her fat arms around me and I thought she was going to hug me to death. When she let me be she said, "My Gerry didn't get his letters…"

I'd given them to Freddie. I'd called the barracks and asked them to send someone round to collect them. The boys going to and coming from the Leb did so on rotation: in three chalks over three weeks. Alex was coming home on the last, so the new lads going out brought stuff to him and the others. I'd wanted him home on the first chalk but he said the extra money would come in handy. I couldn't argue with him on that score. But now I often wish I had.

●

The army took us out there last year. By us, I mean the families of those who had been murdered. They brought us to the actual scene during the day but I insisted on being there in the evening, at the time it happened. So an officer brought us to the bridge when it was night and he had the sense to leave me and Jamie alone with each other. It was dark and a cool breeze stirred the fronds on the road verge. The silhouette of the crusader castle on the hill was darker than the night skies. Jamie said nothing. He smoked, holding his cigarette the same way his dad used to, sheltered by his palm, warming his lifeline perhaps.

●

I'd fallen asleep on the sofa and woke sometime in the middle of the night. The TV was still on, all grey and fuzzy and ringing signal. I lay there, touched my belly. The telly lighting the room in a bluish light, a Bush telly that Alex joked about: "Are we watching the Bush tonight—what's the reception like?" Laughing goodo then at the wit of himself, my hand sliding over to adjust his aerial.

I was thinking about lots on the sofa, wide awake, wondering why that Freddie hadn't given the letters to the lads. He was very quiet and had a way of looking at you when he had drink on him, not what he'd want to do with you, something more: he would want to do that with you and much more besides. Alex didn't like him, just said there was something about him. I got up and turned off the telly and then made tea and brought the cup to bed and put it on the bedside locker where it remained, untouched.

I was up early, feeling fresh in myself, really fresh considering I hadn't slept too well. When I heard the doorbell I thought, 'The rent man's early,' and went to answer. I remember walking the hallway, my hand arced on my back, feeling like an elephant, opening the door to clear Dublin skies and an army officer and a chaplain. They didn't have to open their mouths to tell me—their presence said everything.

One said, "Sorry," and this was the last thing I heard as the roars of me silenced all else they had to say. All that stuff, the bare facts, came later, and even then, they had to pierce a numbness.

•

This bastard who pulled the trigger left my son with a photograph for a father, a few scenes in a videocassette, and a green combat jacket on a wire hangar in a wardrobe. He lives in a gaol and whenever they write or speak of early release for him my stomach rises to my throat, for how could anyone even consider freeing a scum who murdered four young men in cold blood, and even put the gun to the head of one to finish him off? How could they? Do they think that a person forgets? That because I've moved on and remarried and had more children, that it's alright? That I've got over it? That I'm grand, so I am? In some ways they are as bad as the scum who killed Alex, for I think they have his same lack of sensitivity and respect for the lives of others. But I will never forget. I see Alex every day; feel the goodbye kiss, the sad smile, the tears in his eyes, hear the promises on his lips, read the "love you and kisses" in his badly written letters.

I spit on the image in the newspaper photograph and then I take a scissors to the page, cutting around the edges, resisting the temptation to slice through him. I bring the cutting to the sink and place it in the enamel basin and set a match to a corner; watch the flame consume his face, watch as he disintegrates into floating black motes. And then I run the tap and watch the flow of water break the scorched remnants of burned newspaper, and hurry them down the drain.

Jessica Perreault–Howarth

La Nationale

(an excerpt)

24 June 2008
Fête Nationale du Québec

We've been walking for ages, or so it seems, and still it's hard to tell where we'll end up. This was my idea. Tyler is on the verge of some kind of sentiment: frustration, fear, anger; I can hear them all tumbling in his head like shoes in the dryer. I turn, craning my neck to see how far we've come. The crowd continues to seep from the mouth of the Pie-IX metro station, proceeding in an uninterrupted mass up the steep road. The scene reminds me of a book I read as a child, about caterpillars that climbed one on top of the other to form a tower, having heard that they might discover something fantastic at the top, only to be eaten by birds once they got there. Or something to that effect. We walk on in silence. We have never had much to say to each other. I know the shape of his navel and the location of the birthmark on his thigh, but we are not together in any strict sense.

"You don't belong here any more than I do," he says finally. He has decided on anger. I say nothing.

Spirits are high, faces are painted, flags are flying, no one is too drunk yet. Small children ride on the shoulders of their fathers, like little corks temporarily keeping a volatile substance at bay. I imagine that as the day progresses and sunlight wanes, the anger of ordinary men will emerge. Men, music, pride, politics and plastic cups of Labatt's beer. But it's chilly for late June in Montreal; it doesn't feel like summer without the heavy, oppressive humidity that permeates the flesh until it turns people inside out, if only for some shade. Maybe not the kind of weather ripe for conflict. We keep to ourselves nonetheless. Maybe we'll even slouch, Tyler and I, head and shoulders bent slightly, as though we are crossing the border between east and west illegally.

"You can't even speak French," I say, some time later, having decided on obstinacy for myself. He says nothing.

At the top of the hill, the crowd rounds the corner onto Sherbrooke Street, flanking the Olympic Stadium on its north side. The wide road is blocked off in both directions, allowing the crowd to fan out and gather into smaller formations as they continue their march. Street performers belt Felix Leclerc and Jean Leloup songs over acoustic guitars; vendors flog ice cream and hockey jerseys and fleur-de-lys umbrella hats. Tyler takes my hand, laces his fingers in mine. His palm feels warm and conciliatory.

"I've never been this far east on Sherbrooke Street," he says, staring up at the Stadium's west-leaning tower, its base only a hundred feet to our right. I reclaim my hand and tuck it in the back pocket of my jeans.

"Neither have I."

"The largest inclined structure in the world, what a joke," he muses, bringing his forsaken hand up to shield his eyes from the sun. "It looks pretty ramshackle from this side, doesn't it? Must be the underbelly."

Several large panels are missing from the tower's exterior, exposing the bare cement beneath. The paneling that remains is weather-beaten, its dull grey and beige paint peeling off in jagged swaths. A group of teenagers sits on a lawn beneath the tower, drinking cans of beer and laughing loudly. I pause in the immense shadow it casts over Sherbrooke Street to light a cigarette.

By the time we reach the entrance to the event site, we can hear music and cheering through the thick row of maples. I see Tyler recoil slightly at the edge of my vision, but I walk ahead and he follows. Skinny police cadets search bags at the gate, each one proceeding with the timidity of a virgin learning to unhook a bra. I expose the contents of my purse to a doe-eyed, latex-gloved boy of no more than nineteen. Aside from my wallet and cell phone, I have a dozen or so packs of Gauloises, empty and crushed save for one. There is a pocket-sized copy of the Bible that was given to me in the metro station, and a smattering of McDonald's fries, fugitives from their grease-stained packaging. The boy's face twitches as he waves me through.

I sit under a tree while Tyler gets us beer, and I pretend that I am alone. I pretend that I am waiting for someone else, someone named Marc-Antoine or Guillaume, someone writing a thesis on Sartre or Descartes, someone who has been a peacekeeper in Bosnia or a schoolteacher in the Yukon, someone who has been hit by a rubber bullet or Tasered at a G8 conference. I pretend that this day is the catharsis of my oppressed political soul.

"I bet you see yourself as some kind of anthropologist in all this." Tyler hands me a beer and a hot dog and sits against the broad tree trunk.

"I don't want to be an anthropologist. Anthropologists have to be impartial."

"Would you rather be that guy?" He points to a heavyset man drunkenly dancing nearby, wearing only a fleur-de-lys-patterned Speedo and flip-flops.

"Sure." The man gyrates ardently, tripping over his flip-flops and spilling most of his beer in the grass. "That's pretty authentic."

"Fuck off, Cass. That's a *stereotype*. This whole day is a stereotype. This is nationalism on acid, for Chrissake." I can't help but laugh at us both, even though he isn't paying attention.

After a few more drinks, we wander over to the main stage, through a maze of food stalls and beer tents and families sprawled on blankets. The sun emerges and it seems simply that a few thousand people have decided that it's a nice day to be in the park. A huge crowd has gathered around the stage, swaying and dancing and flying their flags. The music is a kind of reggae-hip-hop hybrid with a few multicultural bits thrown in for the occasion. A tolerant, multicultural society: that's the theme the organizers are going for. Tolerant and multicultural, so long as you aren't Canadian, I think, wishing I hadn't thought it at all.

The name of the group is vaguely familiar, something from the new wave of Quebec pop culture that's easy to avoid or ignore if you're Anglo. There are about ten of them on stage, all wearing Montreal Canadiens hockey jerseys. (I had worried, before the referendum in '95, that the Canadiens would have to change their name if Quebec separated from Canada.) The playoffs didn't go well this year; a second round loss to Philadelphia in May ended all talk of getting the Cup back to the city that wanted it most. When we beat Boston in the first round and things looked good, hundreds had rioted in the streets, ebullient and drunk, looting and burning and defacing, just like they had when we last won the Cup, back in '93. They rioted and I stayed home with a bottle of cheap wine and the door bolted shut. But now we're all left with a bleak, fifteen-year void of defeat, stretching itself out in an otherwise storied history.

The group's lead singer, short, muscled and keyed up, addresses the crowd in his French *joale* over the backdrop of a synthesized beat, prodding at collective wounds.

"We're tired!" he shouts, and the people cheer and scream.

"We're tired of losing the Cup!" They scream louder.

"We're tired of losing the referendums!"

"We're tired of this fake fucking country!"

"We...are...the Nation!"

A shockwave runs through the crowd, which rocks and sways and undulates in its intoxication. I feel the vibration in the tips of my fingers, clenching and unclenching my fists.

"Yeah, yeah. *Vive le Quebec libre*. Is that what you wanted to hear?" Tyler is not impressed. "Can we go now?"

On the way back we press together in the crowded metro car, chest to chest. I watch the dim reflection of our embrace in the window. We look like sleepwalkers who have lost their way. In these moments we allow ourselves to be lovers, if only for a point of reference. Just below the hem of my shirt, his index finger circles my hipbone and his thumb presses into the flesh beneath the waistband of my jeans. I feel his breath, heavy on my neck, the beginnings of a whisper. There is nothing to say. He inhales sharply as I slip my hand down the front of his pants. We kiss, lips barely moving in silent ventriloquism. The metro car smells of sawdust and cigarettes, and I can't help but think vaguely of something or someone else. We pull apart and brace ourselves against momentum as the train stops and the doors bang open.

"Is this us?" he asks. I shake my head.

"Next one." We watch as a pale wisp of a woman runs down the stairs onto the platform, a second too late. The doors shut, and she remains frozen there until the train disappears into the darkness of the tunnel.

"So I'm thinking of going to Toronto in August," he says. "I got into the MBA at York."

"I see."

"Come with me, Cass."

"Why would I do that?" He grabs me by the hips and pulls me hard against him.

"What the fuck else is there to do?"

I rest my head on his shoulder as though we might dance.

1 July 2008
Canada Day

My mother checks her watch. That's all right, she doesn't have to be here, *here* in a spiritual sense at least. He wasn't her husband, hadn't been her husband in over twenty years. She comes with me every year so that I won't have to be alone in front of his headstone, invoking a ghost with grocery-store flowers and furtive tears. But for a variety of reasons we're late this year, twenty-two days late, and I'm not crying, and instead of flowers I have three rolls of hockey tape in my hands, *bleu, blanc, rouge*. I place them at the base of the stone in that order. Fifteen years and twenty-two days later, my mother has places to be and things to do, and I am teetering on the brink of an emotion that is neither sadness nor nostalgia, and could very well be the wretched afterbirth of a hangover. It was probably inappropriate of me to have been drinking last night. There was a feeling of cruel subversion to the whole evening, a simmering undercurrent setting the floors at an angle. I lower myself into a crouching ball of nausea at the thought. My mother interprets this as grief and backs away a step.

"Take your time, honey," she says, shifting her weight from left to right, flapping the skirt of her dress so it won't stick to her clammy legs.

I study my Chuck Taylors for a long moment, rub at a stain on the toe, pull at one end of the shoelace until its bow collapses. I press my palm into the grass, dig the tips of my fingers into the cool earth until dirt creeps up under my nails. The headstone is beginning to show its age. Its Zambonied ice-surface luster has dulled over fifteen long winters. The etchings, however, remain clear and distinct. *Gregory James Ferris. 1960-1993. Beloved father, son, friend.* Simple, to the point. What more can you say on a headstone without veering into cliché? Even 'beloved' is probably over-sentimental. He is beloved to me, albeit in the freeze-frame memories of my nine-year-old self. At the time of his death he was unemployed and deeply in debt; it's difficult to say whether or not he was beloved in the eyes of his long-suffering mother and his few friends. I retie my shoe with a double knot and stand up.

"Let's go."

"You sure?"

"I'm sure."

"Do you want to say anything?"

Nausea radiates through my midsection and I stumble a step sideways. My mother has not mentioned the pungent smell of alcohol that is surely seeping from my pores. This is perhaps one of many details to be noted and filed away as she builds her case against me. On what charges I can't decide. Cosmic irony? Tactless melancholy? I am gripped by a sudden urge to swathe my father's headstone with the tape that lies at my feet, to wrap *blue, blanc, rouge* around and around and around until the words and numbers have been obscured.

"Later, Dad."

We walk slowly through the humidity, back onto a gravel path that ends in a set of towering black gates. Afternoon traffic careens down the hill on Côte-des-Neiges just beyond, and we pause at the cemetery's threshold, unsure of whether we will head in the same direction. I fish through my purse for a pack of cigarettes that isn't empty, my mother frowning at me. Normally I abstain from smoking in front of her, but on days like this I am half an orphan, saturated in the sins of my father, smoking being the least of them. She reaches over and takes a cigarette for herself, then walks over to a wooden bench beneath a massive maple tree. I follow, and we sit in silence for a moment, smoking and sighing and sweating.

"Do you have somewhere to be?" I bring the tip of the cigarette up close to my face to watch the paper turn to ash.

"Canada Day barbeque," she answers after a moment. "With Jeff's company."

"Jeff." I enjoy pronouncing my stepfather's name as I exhale so that it emerges as a long sound in diminuendo. He and my mother have been married for two years, and to the man's credit he feels no compunction to play the role of surrogate father. He has no children of his own and comes off as slightly gay, but I have kept this observation to myself. My mother seems happy enough. At the age of forty-five, she has finally found the kind of man who has a nice house in Westmount and drives a car with leather seats and comes home at a reasonable hour without the proverbial lipstick on his collar, although if she's checking for lipstick she might be on the wrong trail. She goes to Tahiti for her winter vacation and I get a nice apartment rent-free in the Plateau. We're grateful, and that's all that's required of us, really. We're familiar with gratitude, my mother and I, and see that it's awarded where due.

"Do you want to come with me?" she asks, knowing that I'll decline, which I do. My phone vibrates at the bottom of my purse, and I reach in to silence it.

"Tyler wants us to drive to Ottawa for the concert and the fireworks and all that."

"Still stringing that boy along, are we?" My mother uses the royal *we* when giving morality lectures, saying things like *we're not impressed* in a tone that doesn't quite take itself seriously. She knows Tyler well enough; he was the boy next door back in the bad old days. In her books, such people are not to be trifled with, just as she would not put her grandmother's china in the dishwasher.

"He knows how it is."

"How is it?"

"Can we not talk about this today? Or ever?" I crush my cigarette into the ground and reach for another, placing it between my lips so that it bounces as I speak. "I do what I can."

"I know." She has finished her cigarette and has nothing to do with her hands other than to twist her wedding band. "It's hot, isn't it?"

"Are we going to talk about the weather now?"

"Well, Christ, I don't know what to say about all this any more." Her exasperation is meek and flat. She takes a shallow breath; the coming reprimand will surely lag in the heat. "You smell like he used to. What, Jack Daniel's? Johnnie Walker? Not very ladylike."

I cradle my head in both hands, the cigarette jutting out like a burning horn. Then the tears come, appearing as conveniently as water in a swimming pool I had always assumed was empty but dove into nonetheless. She places her hand lightly against the small of my back.

"I suppose genetics are working against you," she whispers, as I convulse beneath her fingers.

The storm of self-pity subsides quickly enough, and I wipe mascara from my cheeks. My mother's hand moves in slow, halting circles over the dampness of my back. Humidity sits next to us on the bench, heat bugs scream in our ears.

"I can skip the barbeque," she proposes, "and we could go to a movie. Or the museum or somewhere with air-conditioning." I imagine the phone call she would have to make if I agreed. *I'm sorry Jeff…Cass needs me. Bring me home a piece of cake.*

"No. You should go to your thing. I'll go to Ottawa with Tyler." She sighs at this, although it's probably the response she wants. "Gotta stand by our men," I add, drawling.

"What's Tyler driving these days?" she asks. "I ran into his mother last month and she told me he was working for some Internet company. Must be good money in that."

"I don't know. I'll see you, Mom." I slip on a pair of sunglasses and we kiss goodbye. She remains on the bench as I walk through the gate and down Côte-des-Neiges.

Michael Wynne

Bastard Sister

(an excerpt)

She watches the boy, knowing he watches the other one. She smiles to affectionately think that he, the first one, is her rival, one for whom, in her possibly greedy way, she harbours desire, also. There just below her, his body slightly rocks, but as if he revels in a controlled kind of restlessness more than in response to the music that fills the room. Beneath the too-strong light, the blond of his riot of hair looks aggressively fake. His close-fitting shirt is a faded red and has a springing lizard on the back.

The other, older, boy holds himself motionless in his tailored blazer. He faces the young wide-breasted singer, who makes valiant eye contact with the crowd as she croons on the low platform before them. His posture is at once attentive and laid-back, and his ringed hands are at his sides. In the left is the phone he's just been checking. The fingers of the right are gripped around the mouth of a glass of whiskey poured the only way she knows he'll take it, large and neat.

When the music breaks, she sees the pair sidle closer toward one another. Her thick-lined eyes freeze like a mask's. At her ear someone says in a sham rasping voice that she looks lovely. Lovely is a word she hates. She rounds on whoever says it, as if reacting to a slight. Under the ugly light looms a mauvely lip-sticked, teasing face she knows like it's her own. The lipstick twitches and thins in a smile that says, "Kiss me, Serena." Kiss me are words that don't need repeating; but she repeats them anyway, saying, "Kiss me a big birthday girl kiss." For a second the girls' tongues come together like palms pressed in prayer; then, one after the other, those tongues sink like sinners unsaved in each wide-open mouth that moulds itself over the other.

Who laughs then, as the girls ease apart—one of themselves, or one of those clear-voiced boys who have been watched? The latter, it seems. From here Serena realises she hears the clearer voice of the two ask, "Who'd bother killing someone with a bloody beer keg? There are quicker ways. And less strenuous."

When the girls separate, both pairs of eyes slide knowingly across each cleft-chinned face. The girl whose chin-cleft is slighter is self-styled Darina, a word she wears as a pendant that hangs in gold above the square neck of her dress. Laughing, she says, unprompted, "The bastard hates it."

"The play?"

The mauve mouth makes a moue that asks, What else?

"Why, what's his gripe with it?"

"Who cares?" Darina sighs, her eyes languid on the crowd, one wide shoulder quickly rising and falling.

"Well, exactly."

"Still, his problem with it is…"

"Yeah?"

"It lacks a twist."

"A *twist*?"

"I reckon he was messing," Darina understates, and insists, "I argued anyhow that it's twisted enough," out of a mouth you could describe as being, humorously, in the same condition. Then through an angled straw she takes a slow draw of an amythest-coloured brew she holds loosely, and adds, "Overall, he got bent out of shape about it. Said it was bitter for the sake of it."

A blast of ammonia surrounds them as two other girls spill giggling through the dragged-in door of the toilet to their right. One calls, "Cool play, Darina," and adds so she can be heard, "That's yer one that done *Violence in Smithfield*."

Taking no notice, Darina says, "Only *he* could breed doubts in my mind."

"When he's not reading it, you mean?"

"Yes." The two lean in together, laughing thrilled, sympathetically soundless laughs. "Isn't it mad how he knew I was transitioning, going only on his wife's description of me—isn't it weird? He said he *felt* it. *Transitioning*—the very word he used. He came out with all this the first night he walked me back from Stoneybatter. I think I was just relieved he spoke—that he wasn't forever stuck in that dominating silence of his. There was this amazing calm and this confidence about him that was so different it made me want to possess him. I mean it, Serena. Then the card he sent me when I was recovering— did I mention it?—with some lines from Cavafy in it: that clinched it, if nothing else did. You could say I'm obsessed. I'd forgive him anything— even his not showing up tonight."

"You're still into him, I gather?"

Elegantly, Darina's eyes roll several inches above the level of the other's, and the mauve of her mouth contracts in a smile of concerted self-insight. "I suppose you could say I'm like Emily Dickinson, in one way at least—silent men scare me stiff. But yeah, I'm *into* him. He's more or less my exact type—an oddball brain-box with the bod of a drill sergeant. Did I tell you his wife says that when he can't sleep, instead of counting sheep he constructs the geographies of South America and Africa?"

"She'd know."

"None better," agrees Darina, with a bitterness that is only half put on. "I thought she was a nut, going on about his second sight the minute she hired me. I *hated* him before I met him. Then when he appeared in the shop one night I was instantly, well, *taken*. Now *there's* a man, I thought. I drink this mainly because it reminds me of him." Her lips seize the straw, release it after a beat. "Both men and women swear he's the best sex. And then, the rumours add to his mystique— that he's into black magic, that he strangled a man. Who wouldn't be smitten, or inspired?"

"Can't imagine. You saw his brother here?"

"Pascal? Where? Oh, there. Yes, I *thought* that was his voice a minute ago."

"Actually, that was the other one's voice."

"What other one?"

"The blond in the red. Pascal's new paramour, I'm thinking."

"Oh. You jealous?"

"Yes." After a second she adds, despite herself, "But I want them both."

Their laughter has the low note of relished grievance, as of those who have known equally what it is to submit to the devil of rejection. The mauve of Darina's lips reaches down to meet the other's cheek, then withdraws, and encloses itself on the angled straw. Thick-lined eyes switch from the raised drink which the use of the straw slightly depletes that moment, and from the drinker, whose tall form, having retreated into the harsh-lit corner that to sensitive noses smells faintly of vomit, now stands as if absorbed in a private world that annuls all others; and those eyes hold on the two boys, who now stand close to the edge of the dance space, their heads the width of a fist apart. Leaving Darina, she descends a few steps, among a necking couple and a braying group. When she's just behind them, she hears one of the boys say through a good-natured laugh, "They say she's a child prodigy," and to this the immediate reply, "Well, they sure got the first part right."

They turn as if unsurprised when she says, "Having fun dissecting someone?" and she holds in her own the stare of the older one as he wonders, "Well, Serena—here with your soul sister?"

"She's just behind you and can practically hear your every word, you tossers."

Over their shoulders they throw unrepentant and affectionately indifferent grins at her, and beyond, toward the odorous corner.

"Ah, but she's out of it on that poison she's on—Black Witch, or whatever the hell she calls it. She is, isn't she?—if I know Darina," adds the older, be-ringed boy, a nearly middle-aged man really, with an oval, subtle-bearded face whose handsomeness is as lasciviously crow-footed and eternal as Pan's. "And," he quietly laughs, "I *know* Darina. Almost as well as you do yourself."

"You probably do. You certainly *inspire* her. You and that notorious brother of yours." The blue of an angled spotlight above them can be seen to be curiously alien to the duskish blue of her eye—a shade it fails to play on as she gives him a broad wink.

"Whatever about her inspiration, Pascal's having trouble persuading me her play's up to scratch," the boy in faded red admits. When he speaks, his long-crowned head sways, then halts, and, despite what he's said, there is a warm and erotic kind of humility in that smile of his that shows teeth discoloured with weakness. It is true she is repulsed by that smile, or some vague, unwanted part of her is, even as she is aroused by it. She likes the thought of tasting what repels a prudish part of her.

At last, Serena admits in turn, "According to Darina, Pascal's sibling thinks the same as you do, for a different reason, maybe—whether he inspires her, or not."

"But part of the idea came straight from him," the blond reminds her. "Or so Pascal tells me."

"Yes. Well, partly from him, partly from me. But it seems it's the play's *tone* that bothers him, Greg."

"Its tone? He actually came out and said that?"

"He did." Serena smiles. "He's known to open his mouth, on occasion. Anyhow, what I think is, it's basically her *originality* that irks him. That, and her youthful energy."

In response, Greg's blond, longish head slightly sways its length again, and their eyes hold and blend in a strange, expressive, superbly mutual recognition. Does he remember she has seen him erect? The warmth of his ugliness intrigues her, and could possibly trick her—and many—into love. She almost hates the way his upturned, thin-septumed nose makes his face, when eyed from certain angles, become lost in a nostril-abyss.

Excluded for the time-being, their heavy-ringed friend sips and sips his whiskey. As he sips, the weirdly pure whites of his eyes roll in the blue light. She—Serene, as he calls her—senses them roll. The wide-breasted, sequinned body of the singer takes to the performers' space as she glances at him and says, "Pascal," with an ironic urgency. She adds, before the music begins again, "What you said is so."

"What?"

"What you said is right."

"About…?" The amber in the glass raised close to his face dulls the stout opal on his index.

"She believes in brutality, just like you said. Philosophically speaking, that is."

"Who does? Darina?" Greg almost annoys her by butting in.

"*Believes in brutality*—did I say that?" laughs Pascal, lowering the glass and raising his phone, which sounds a siren tone. His head dips, as if in modest triumph, and he moves away from them, speaking amused, low words. Serena, enjoying jealous qualms, watches; then, her back stiff, she turns and eyes the singer roll her hips as she sings *I Committed Murder*.

A stranger at her shoulder complains of a whiff of puke at the back of the room at the same moment Greg asks, "Haven't I seen you and Darina snogging?"

"Ah, we're always at that crap," she says, "for the craic. Aren't we soul sisters, as Pascal says."

"And of course you were next door earlier?"

"At the play? I was, yeah. Half the audience is here."

"Is it true you knew the dead man she used for the story?"

Her eyes stay on the singer when she replies, "Know him? No. We fucked once, that's all…Speaking of fucking, are you keen on having Pascal?"

"*Having* him?" His weak teeth bite back a laugh at her phrasing.

Not caring, she insists, "You are, aren't you?"

He keeps his eyes on the singer also as he says, "Darling, you're a bit behind. Myself and Pascal—"

He stops and, when he checks, Serena's eyes are on him. He cannot resist what he sees, but would not articulate seeing, there in their glazed jadedness, where guilty lust, something close to fledgling hate, and understanding seem to do semi-lethargic battle. "My God," he begins, almost nervous, "you're getting mad—or *are* mad at, at—"

"No," she interrupts. "No. I'm not." Her head moves in slow negation. "But tell me, what's that reptile on your back meant to represent? Or need I ask?"

In confused, unhurt amusement, his humble grin grows, and he chooses to be silent. Quickly, she kisses his grin, arresting it. "Never mind. You know I love you both to bits."

"Both of us?" she smiles to hear him repeat; while, nearby, the same complaining voice declares, "That fat cunt is murdering that fucking number."

That second, Pascal reappears, and both men stand shoulder to shoulder before her again. Pascal announces, "I reckon Darina's ready to go."

"I think she's got the urge," Serena says; "whether she's out of it, or not."

"Urge?" they both echo.

"To write something."

"What drives her, you'd wonder," says Pascal, fondly ironic.

"The truth." Loyally, Serena refuses to take up his attitude.

"The truth? Darina?" His laugh comes out harsh, as if out of an ache of disbelief.

"Yes: telling the truth about people. She says it's the only good reason to write."

The room for a split second seems subdued by that laugh of his when it clangs louder and as disbelieving-sounding as before. "If there's a nobler goal or credo," he pretends to concede, "I'm blessed if I know of it."

"You sound as bitter as your brother believes Darina is."

"Bitter—Darina? No. Vindictive, maybe."

At this Serena has to laugh. "That's nice, and on her birthday and everything."

"Her birthday?" Greg asks.

"Yeah, she's just turned twenty—too old to be a *child* prodigy, I'd say." She sees how Greg notices when she nudges Pascal.

"Greg reckons she's young for her age—in *some* ways…"

"So I understand." She turns to their friend in red, but with a nod he is escaping to the bar— "To get our favourite prodigy a birthday beverage, no doubt," Pascal grins, and adds, "Looks like Darina's racking up the reasons to celebrate—her birthday, the play, her surgery…And so now she's Darina *officially*, at last, hmm?"

"She's been Darina officially for some time."

"I've never asked her why *that* name? Because it nearly rhymes with yours, maybe?"

"Happens she always liked it. Even when she was a little boy."

"For as long as you've known one another, so."

"For as long as we've known one another," Serena confirms.

"And what sort of a kid was she?"

"What you'd expect—a cheeky wee bastard, with a tongue like a switchblade."

For a minute they appear to listen to *Strange Fruit* being sung. Pascal stands erect and a little in front of Serena, with his chin jutting forward over his whiskey glass toward the stage. This rendition is better than previous efforts and Serena is moved in believing Pascal to be appreciative—even, perhaps, transported. In this state he strikes her as cheerfully isolated and exposed. She wonders if he senses the heavy accusation of her lust. Even to hear him inhale energetically makes her shoulders tauten with desirous, fathomless jealousy. Right now she attends more to his listening than anything. At the same time it pleases Serena to find the performer's body revolting, a pleasure that is strengthened by the latter's clearly innocent desire to entertain. She coldly asks herself why it is we often want to attack others for sharing something that we both love. Her own question fails to interest her, however. On a low note the singer's throat seems to bulge like a bullfrog's. As if it's a trick, someone close by applauds, cheers. Serena secretly sneers and fends off boredom. She doesn't have to move an inch to know that by now Darina's gone. There is no holding that one once she is inspired, which she likes to say she often is.

Serena was at first aghast at the level of her envy at Pascal's incisiveness when it came to his guessing Darina's good-in-evil premise; but she is now over it—being appalled as well as envious, that is. For, as Darina has explained in her city-centre bedroom on a recent sozzled night as sultry as this one, brutality and vileness are *necessary* for goodness to exist, which is the kind of thing Pascal is tickled to think she expresses less out of passionate conviction than a wish to impress. In any case, she hoped when the time came Serena would see that the play was concerned not so much with this notion, nor with the murderously violent incident (involving a beer keg) of its title, than with how all good friends revile and even hate each other on some secret level and wish in one form or another for one another's death. Serena remembers her saying how hate of this special, clandestine, binding kind is friendship's fuel, keeps friendship going busily—something she described with a smile impressive for its uncertainty. By Serena and others she's been heard to say this theory of hers ties in with some philosopher's idea about the terrifying realities we spend our lives dodging. Serena knows it is only when Darina's pissed that she can be spurred to talk like this.

It is clear when Greg is back that he himself is pissed. He greets her by gripping a buttock she wishes he didn't release so soon. The song that seems to have entranced Pascal is over and as another song starts he moves away to take another call. Before he disappears in the crowd, that disbelieving laugh of his discharges, setting off subtle smarts through Serena's vitals. By the time, a minute later, Greg mentions something about his van parked off the alley, the complexion of her mood is recast, and it seems to her there's no more logical place to be. His fingers respect the way her arm resists them as the two of them leave by a side door. In the back of his van she orders, "Say nothing; just sit on my face," and he obeys without a word, without even a smirk. She takes pains to make him lower himself in such a way that, while her throat grips the head of his dick, she can catch faintly the essence of his unwashed arsehole—which makes her think, with a tender half-resentment, of bad corn.

Rosaleen McDonagh

Consanguinity

In-breds Hurlers syndrome
Rickets disease
Mental Health Disability.

Choices versus values and norms
Often bodies produced
In unusual aesthetic forms
Length, breadth and size.

The spirit, the essence of our ethnicity can't be traced.
The Myths,
The Famine—
Sagas of Irish history
That should be replaced.
Nomadism a journey
We once trekked.

Bad blood
Double-first cousins
Keep the family ties.
Be-questioned,
Be-quizzed—
Let them judge
Our cultural survival,
Can't be for outsiders to fudge.

Knowledge and power
Are put far from our reach,
A settled Irish agenda
Is all that they teach.

They tell us about our genes—
Recessive, too similar
But these rare defaults
Are not always found in the familiar,
Whom do we trust?
Every angle, every answer
Is alien to us.

Anthropologists, Medics and Physicists chirp their
Chimes as a way of assimilating us.
Often we can't get checked,
The gene-pool is small.
Our morality—what's the fuss?
It's what defines us.
Research and data say
Don't marry too close—

We know something older
Good sense
The Father, Son, and Mary most Holy Ghost.

Vanity

When I threaten to leave you
You trap me to stay.
No effort, no thought—you're lazy with sloth
Manipulation is the game you play.

You fail me in ways
With no hint to change
Clumsy inappropriateness—
You're unwilling to rearrange.

Knotted and twisted
Burnt with rage—
Your strength
I'm afraid to gauge.

Making outrageous demands
Which seem unfair—
Teasing and flirting
Pretending you care.

My body is old—
Too stiff to move
My empty torso.
You have stolen its groove.

You're no longer shiny, clean or sharp
Quick, fast or first
A subservient intellect
You're an incurable thirst.

My muscles my bones my flesh
My body my mind.
Pride hasn't spared
Sporadic bursts of energy.

Dulcet tones—now grumpy and slow
On hearing lies, of wanting to seek help
Often the sound of your voice
I no longer know—

The one that promised elegance
Packed with poise
Ego carrying false decadence
Now seems ambitious for any womanly relevance.

Now filled with silence—
The shame has set in
Our space—once shared.
Only I inhabit your sin.

A shadow—
A mask—I replaced
This one beautiful body
Now an aesthetic disgrace.

I'll feed you with Botox
Pump you with iron till I sweat.
Ageing with grace
A virtue that isn't yours yet.

I can inject you with pride
And more self-esteem
But my credit card has become spent
With these useless treatments I've grown mean.

Intimacy—secrets or plans—
Elements of love we no longer share
My broken confidence
You intrude on every sphere.

I ignore you for a moment
For a rest—a fantasy or fling—
Like a bad lover
My Cerebral Palsy, my Vanity.
I'm unable to leave you
My silly old thing.

Declan Gorman

Airport Roundabout

Harvo stands on the flyover above the M1 at Swords, his crossbow pulled taut and aimed at the road below. Next red car along gets it. A blue Mercedes speeds towards him and passes underneath. Motionless, he waits. Now comes a silver Toyota hatchback. Now blue again, this time a Mazda. In the distance a red car. Oh gift! A Lexus Coupe Convertible, roof down! It nears. A woman driver.

"Die, bitch!"

He releases the trigger, the bolt flies down in a true line, passes just above the woman's head, skids off the boot and hits the road behind. She doesn't even notice.

"Shite!" says Harvo, and heads off home for his tea.

•

The woman drives on, Deborah Rowe, from Skerries. She is listening to REM on her iPod Touch. She sings along, the warm wind in her face, late afternoon, early May.

"That's me in the corner. That's me in the spotlight, losing my religion."

She turns off the M1, up the slipway and on down to the airport roundabout, casting a glance out of habit at John Kindness' aeronautic artwork. It means nothing to her. The coupe purrs up the ramp and glides into the short-term. Debbie parks, slings her Louis Vuitton across her shoulder and walks briskly towards the Arrivals Hall to meet her husband, Roddy.

•

Roddy's plane is delayed. In fact, as Roddy well knows, it's in trouble, big fucking trouble! Oh, he can read between the lines, hearing beneath the calm voice of the pilot the true panic he knows is gripping the cockpit.

"We are just awaiting clearance to land," announces Captain Cronin or whatever the guy said his name was.

"We have just lost another engine," Roddy hears.

He reclines his middle seat, no one either side of him. The plane is half-empty, maybe only fifty passengers. He'd rather have died with three hundred others on a Jumbo. He's the only white man aboard. The Jumbo is flying from Harare to Copenhagen. A terrorist attack. His name will be in the papers. He will get an obituary in the *Irish Times*. Leading finance executive at the peak of his career. But no, this is Aer Lingus from Gatwick and he's flying home for the weekend, like every weekend, after his four-day week's work with Ernst & Young Accounting, his fear of flying as acute now as it was the first time he flew at age twelve on a school tour to Paris and puked. Therapy no help. Pills no help. Ease back in the seat. Get me down, Cronin or Crowley or whatever your name is, you slow bastard!

The flight attendant passes along and asks him to return his seat to the upright position. Roddy obliges, while staring the bitch out.

"See you in Hell...Marie!" he thinks, as she glides on past him, "We're going down together."

Old habit. He always checks out one of the stewards' names. He notes it during the take-off safety routine. Could put you ahead of the queue if the worst were to happen. "Sorry, Marie isn't it? Could you help me down the chute...I have this leg thing..." He looks out the window as the plane plummets to earth.

"At least we'll take out Swords."

He swigs from his mineral water, one last mouthful of Kerry Spring before facing the Devil. He glances across at an African woman sitting alone across the aisle, peering out her window at the fields of north Dublin below. His hands sweat. The fields rush at him, the wheels crash against the tarmac, the plane careers along, he suppresses a surge of acid vomit. And then they slow right down and he hears the calming notes of the tinkling piano filtering in on the tinny sound system. And everything is alright again.

Well done, Cronin, he thinks. Well done!

●

Marie O'Connor walks briskly through customs with her colleague Claire. A big wave for Eugene, the security guard. Three days leave now before her next flight. Amsterdam, 6 a.m., Monday. She's growing tired of the job. In Mammy's time an air hostess was seen as the most glamorous job in Ireland, like the lady who pulled the sweepstake ticket on the TV. Now it's just hard work and the pay is only middling and they keep threatening mergers and takeovers and wage cuts and layoffs. And the passengers can be bloody rude, like that sneering guy who reclined his seat as they were touching down.

I could just say yes to Steve, she thinks, settle down, join a gym and a golf club, live in Navan, have kids, grow old.

Claire senses her distance, her unease.

"You coming down to The Castle Saturday?" she asks.

"Huh? No. Not this weekend. Steve is taking me out somewhere to dinner. I think he's gonna ask me to marry him."

"And?"

"I don't know, Claire, I don't know."

●

Eugene watches the two cabin stewards as they merge into the crowd at arrivals. He finds them glamorous, with their neat uniforms and flight bags and polite manners and neat hair. Eugene likes neat. He is neat and natty himself, in his own way. His belly is large, bloated from beer drinking, but his shirt is neatly ironed and tucked in. His beard is neatly plucked, sitting tidily on his large chin, connecting carefully with his trim moustache. His cheeks are clean-shaven, no side-facial hair, no sideboards, just a tidy beard pruned and planted upon on his chin. He likes the airport. Much better than Motorola. Best thing he ever did was to take the Motorola redundancy. Now he is officially Garda-cleared, trained in First Aid and uniformed.

He is betrayed by a sudden moment of lower bowel wind, checks that no one is looking, scratches his arse and farts quietly at the same time. The smell hovers around him a bit longer than usual. He worries someone might come along. Nobody comes. His bowel is at him a lot this past few months, and his arse is constantly itchy. Maybe need to get that looked at. The glass doors open and shut for a Nigerian woman with a trolley full of suitcases. The wind blows the fart away.

•

Oni Adeleke, a resident of Swords, enters the arrivals area, returning from a short visit to her brother in London. Her mood warms when she sees her two daughters, Mojisola and Yetunde waiting at the barrier. She calls out and the two children jump up and down excitedly. Behind them, her older sister Wasola stands smiling broadly and waving, accompanied by her daughter, Blessing, and a white child Oni has never seen before, obviously a friend of Blessing. The white girl stands quietly aside as the others clamour excitedly around Oni, demanding to know what presents she's brought and how was London and how was their uncle. The mothers greet and speak animatedly in Yoruba about their brother's forthcoming marriage, until Blessing glowers at Wasola and both women remember to speak in English before the white girl. Blessing is nine, a delicate age.

"This is Ciara, my friend," she says.

"Hello, Ciara."

"They are on their way to hip-hop," Wasola says. "Come on everybody! Out to the car! Help your auntie with her suitcases."

•

The hip-hop class is located in the function room of a football club in Swords. Thirty kids are already arranged in a V formation as Blessing and Ciara enter.

"Oh no!" Ciara says. "Look. Lara's back!"

"Why do you dislike her so much?" Blessing whispers.

When I grow up, I wanna be famous, I wanna be a star. The sound system thumps out the song and the girls fall into line and go through the dance routine. Two more sessions before summer recess and the concert for the parents.

"Because she smells!"

Blessing spins and sees the whole class spin with her. She loves this moment, the first big spin.

"And five, six, seven, eight. And one, two, three, four."

What Ciara said about Lara was unkind. It is true that Lara smells some days. She smells of wee, but a person can't really help that. Well, she can, of course, by washing. But you can wash away a smell. You can't wash away a bad thought or a bad sin, Mamma says. And Pastor Tiamayu says there are many pitfalls of sin in Swords. If you fall into a pit, you can never climb out without God's forgiveness. At Halloween, Pastor Tiamayu said the children should not go out on the parade because it invoked demons, but Mamma said it was OK so long as you just saw it as a game and didn't actually pray to the Devil. Ciara was not a mean person, usually. She was actually quite brave and had once stood in front of Blessing when some boys from another school had called her bad names and threatened to hit her. But what she said about Lara was unkind.

"And one-more-time!"

Blessing catches sight of her own reflection in the big bar mirror. Her white and pink tracksuit is bright and clean. Mamma bought it yesterday in Penneys. Her hair is up in braids with coloured ribbons.

It took Mamma an hour to do it up for Aunt Oni coming home.

I am a pretty girl, she thinks, and loses herself again in the dance moves. She looks across at Lara. Lara is a good dancer. Her bony arms and shoulders twist in perfect time to the song. Her knees lift in a strange but hypnotic goose step. She is completely engaged in the dance. Blessing smiles at her. Lara looks away, her face sour, looks at the floor.

●

Lara walks home lonely. As she approaches the gate of her house she sees her brother disappear up around the corner of the estate. He is alone and in one of his shuffly moods. She hides behind a car until he is out of sight. In the house, Ma is watching telly.

"There's beans in the kitchen. Make yourself toast," she says, without rising.

"Where's Harvo gone?" Lara asks.

"I dunno. He had his tea."

"What did he have?"

"Beans," Ma says. "Same as you."

"I have a note from hip hop."

She hands her mother the note.

"Two more weeks?" Ma says. "Ah Jaysus. She's lookin' a hundred and sixty euro for next year. That's gone up!"

"Will you come to the concert? Please Ma?" The child tilts her head, imploring.

"Hah? Oh, I will, love. Course I will."

Lara feels great relief. She thinks of hugging her mother but decides not to. She goes into the kitchen. Harvo's half-finished beans and toast are on the draining board. She scrapes the leftovers into the dog's pot, reaches into the breadbin and takes the last two slices of white bread. Tomorrow is Friday and Ma will go to Lidl and buy more. In the gap between the cooker and the press unit she sees a mousetrap her mother had set six months ago, covered in a thick grey cobweb, the bait of bacon-fat untouched, turned green with age.

Harvo goes down to the river behind the warehouse, but no one is around. He kicks away the ashes of a fire and finds two blackened dessert spoons, abandoned by some junkies. A skinny dog appears and Harvo kicks a burnt can in its direction.

"Fuck off, mutt!" The dog cocks its head and slinks away.

Harvo walks. He goes up the main street, quiet now with the shops just closed and before the pubs fill up. A few people are sitting outside Trentuno smoking and drinking coffee. Across the street he sees a copper. The copper watches him. He walks on. He's gonna take a long walk. At the Pavilions Shopping Centre, he sees his reflection all distorted in Mc Cabes' plate glass window. He is wearing his Liverpool jersey, grey sweat pants and new runners. He dribbles, weaves and kicks a pretend ball and then stops himself. Naff! Kids' stuff.

Out on the dual carriageway, the rush hour cars heading north are lined up three lanes deep, hardly moving. Harvo walks among them easily, steps up onto the meridian and waits for his chance to cross the uncluttered southbound carriageway, where the cars are fewer but traveling at high speeds, back towards the city. He looks over his shoulder at the crawling rush hour drivers.

Youse are all goin' the wrong way, he thinks.

He smirks invisibly at his private joke and walks coolly out onto the southbound lane. Cars swerve and horns sound but he walks, doesn't run. Walk, don't run. Walk, don't run.

He walks in the direction of the airport, crossing the grassy Pinnock Hill roundabout, past the Little Chef and then on along the left-hand pavement skirting the Airside Retail Park. The surface car park is still half-full. He thinks he might go into Airside, maybe see if he can get into Smyths' and look at a few games or something, but he knows he won't get past security. He climbs over the fence and wanders down among the parked cars.

In the Harvey Norman Superstore in Airside, Debbie Rowe and Roddy are discussing print cartridges with a Latvian shop assistant.

"No, I don't know the reference number," says Roddy. "I bought the printer here. It's a Cannon."

"Yes," says the assistant, "but which model?"

"I dunno! It's black."

"Not colour?"

"No, it is colour," Roddy says impatiently. "The printer itself is black. The machine is black. The outside of it. The apparatus."

Deborah moves over to one side to look at flatscreen TVs.

•

The 33 bus swings around the airport roundabout and heads north. Eugene sits in the front seat, on the top deck, looking out ahead. The unease in his bowel has settled. He had a bit of relief just before knocking off. A hard stool, he would tell Dr. Rice. Ten minutes straining but a good hard stool. He would go and see him on Saturday. For now, life was good. A Polish chap was due to call by at half-seven to look at the tumble dryer. It had sat for a week in "Buy and Sell" without a single enquiry. Now he had the Polish lad calling and later on a man from Kildare, if the Pole didn't take it straight away.

I won't let it go for less than two hundred, he thinks, and picks up his *Herald* to scan the sports.

•

Marie O'Connor drives away from the Pavilions Shopping Centre in Swords, having bought a few bits and pieces—cosmetics, a top for her date with Steve, a new handbag. At the roundabout, she yields to a big people-carrier driven by a hesitant African woman. The car is full of kids, one of them white. Another African woman is in the front passenger seat, dressed magnificently. Marie follows the big car cautiously, the "L" plate on the rear windscreen a warning to keep her distance.

●

In the Airside carpark, Harvo spots the red Lexus coupe. It's the same one. He goes over to have a gander, to see if his bolt scratched the paintwork. It didn't. He might as well not have fired it. Fuck sake! Then his eye falls on a gift. On the tarmac, smack on the white paint between the parking bays, a set of keys. The bitch dropped her keys. Harvo has never driven before, but he was often in cars with other lads, racing and spinning up at the roundabouts and out on the motorway. He picks up the keys and sits into the driver's seat, the black cushion still carrying the impress of Deborah Rowe's perfect, toned ass. He checks the glove compartment and finds only a deep red MAC lipstick, lid off. It takes him a minute to figure out the basic workings of the car—wipers this side, indicators that, ignition there…and shite…it's an automatic—less of a buzz, but a jammer's a jammer. He reverses out of the bay and drives slowly at first, up towards the main road. At the junction he makes a spur-of-the-moment decision.

"Ya know wa'? I'm gonna go back for me bolt!"

Mad! He swings right and accelerates off northwards back towards the Little Chef, driving on the southbound carriageway, weaving along on the wrong side of the road.

●

The traffic has been stopped for a few minutes now. Eugene eventually looks up from his newspaper to see what's going on. From his lofty perch, he sees the carnage up ahead. He runs down the stairs.

"Let me out," he says to Joe, the driver. "There's an accident up ahead. African woman out on the road hollerin', goin' mad."

"Huh? Is that what it is? And what are ya gonna do, Eugene? Are ya gonna walk home to Lusk from here?"

"No, Joe! I'm trained in First Aid. I'm gonna see if I can help."

Joe pushes the button and the doors hiss open. Up ahead he can hear the anguished screams of a Nigerian woman crying out to Jesus

Christ. Jesus Christ, my Lord and Saviour! You will not allow this! You must not allow this! Jesus Christ, You are my Lord and Saviour!

Joe closes the door again. He leans his elbows on the steering wheel, rests his chin on his cupped hands and watches as portly Eugene races along between the stationary cars, belly bouncing up and down, his jacket swinging in the summer breeze, hitching up his Securicor trousers as he runs to assist with the dead and the injured.

Rahul D'Silva

Frida Kahlo in Coyoacán

My house is filled with monkeys.
Quick like spiders, with nimble fingers,
they confiscate everything in sight.
Here I rust away, floating from
one December to another. The sparrows visit—
little *cheeps* trail my broken foot,
and sometimes the wings of a lost hummingbird
flutter above me like a waking dream.
At least there's no one here to yell
pata de palo, pata de palo...
the monkeys cannot talk. But at night
they are my lost sons and daughters,
until I wake in the searchlight sun
amidst my curious menagerie.

★ *pata de palo, pata de palo*: peg-leg, peg-leg

Notes from India

1. Mangoes

After school each day I ate mangoes
from the street vendor's cart.
Salted, unripe ones—the tart taste
made my lips smack and thirst
for something cold and fizzy.
We weren't supposed to eat such snacks…
Germs! They said. *You'll fall sick!*
When we got home, we ate the sweet ripe ones.
The juice dribbled down our chins.

2. Biryani

On Sundays my grandfather prepared
his special biryani. The smell of cloves
lit up the house, until we couldn't focus
on our games of cards. He made it his way,
spicy and filling, till the day he had a stroke.
In the hospital the blood seeped into his brain
like cardamom wafting into the ceiling.

At Twenty-One

At twenty-one you begin to think
The world doesn't quite make sense any more.
Your friends turn more and more to drink,
Finding pleasure in tipsiness: they say you're a bore.

You search for the words that will validate your toil,
To make sense of the hours you spend locked away.
But your peers don't burn that midnight oil—
They quickly pen sonnets, pass their evenings at play.

Meanwhile you spend days writing in cafés,
Trying to find some inspiration,
But also secretly hoping to taste
That blonde whose soft lips promise salvation.

Where are the women who should be impressed
By men who spend hours crafting a line?
The legion of nymphs who'll take you to bed
Just because you're a poet—for that you're divine.

O Rimbaud, you said no one's serious
At seventeen, when lindens line the promenade.
But you wrote great poems even when delirious,
High on hashish, passed out in the shade.

I'm just trying to find some success
With poetry—and of course women, it's true.
But at twenty-one it's so hard to impress
Anyone, when you're always feeling so blue.

Holt and Hover

at Swarthmore

I can be seen wherever I am standing—
at night watching a hare stiff as a star
or in daytime the shy quivering of a cherry tree in bloom.

When I walk I pay homage to the leaf-dappled light,
the vigilant watchman of the goldfinch flock
and the gnarled puissance of the magnolia trees.

If I stood here long enough,
through the days and nights,
my paws would root deep into the ground.

Ducks

He is jealous, this teal-blue helmeted king:
I am brazenly eyeing his heather-brown queen.

Pictogram

Knit together, exhausted,
one phalanx of limbs—
my penis a sleeping seahorse
curled against your thigh,
your breasts two mangoes
nestled against my chest.

Legos

"And what if the operation goes wrong?" Mummy said. "What then?"

"Well, what other option is there?" Papa said. Mummy had no reply. She went into the bedroom, and Papa sat down in his easy-chair, with a resigned look on his face. Picked up the paper. A slow crackling of the pages, as he turned to the sports section to look at the cricket highlights. "Look, Neil, England beat Pakistan today."

I never knew what to do in these situations. Mummy and Daddy always got along, but lately there were prolonged silences where no one spoke in the house. Mummy seemed different—more sad, more angry, and was always too tired to play with me. It worried me, but when I asked Papa he said these were grown-up things and that I shouldn't worry. So I went back to my drawing book, lying on my stomach on the thick Turkish carpet in the living room. After a while, Papa went into the bedroom.

There were shelves in the living room filled with objects from Papa's travels and gifts from friends. Ivory-carved elephants. Paper fans from Japan. The bottom shelf was mine. In it, arranged carefully for display, were the toys I had received from relatives abroad. I was rarely allowed to play with these, for they were deemed far too valuable for casual use. Every once in a while, under careful super-vision, I was allowed to take them out and examine them, but never really to play with them – especially so with the blue gunmetal trucks. On the rare occasions when I was allowed to handle the trucks, I contented myself with spinning the wheels with the palm of my hand, imagining that the soft whirring was the roar of the truck speeding down the highway.

When Papa came back in the evening, Grandmother was with him, and he had a box under his arm. "I picked her up in town, Neil—she'll be staying for a few days." And after much pleading, he revealed that the box was a set of Legos from my uncle in Dubai. Still, I wasn't allowed to play with them, and no amount of pleading would change his mind. "These are expensive," he said. "You'll scratch them and lose them." Dinner was a quiet meal, uncharacteristically so, for I was used to Papa telling jokes in his booming voice, and Mummy good-naturedly scolding him for using such language in front of me.

The next day, Papa and Mummy left on a trip. They were both dressed up, and there was the heady scent of shoe polish in the air. I liked that smell, because it meant that Papa was going out somewhere special. There were usually gifts when he returned. Mummy bent down and kissed me goodbye, and told me to be a good boy while she was gone. She looked sad. Soon it began to rain.

At lunchtime, Grandmother called me to the table. There was a feast laid out for me. Slightly sour dal, rice, potatoes, and chapattis. The chapattis were a special touch—she knew they were my favourite. And while the potatoes were in big chunks, not the way Mummy would have made them, Grandmother had even made paysam, extra sweet with vermicelli and cashews, just the way I liked it. And I was permitted two helpings that day, a loosening of discipline that I was not used to. Mummy would never have let me eat two bowls.

There was a lull that evening, as the rains wore off. Suddenly, the world came alive again, the night sounds picking up once the gunshot pebbles of raindrops had stopped hitting the roof tiles. I wanted to go out and collect worms in a tin can and watch them squirm all over each other. But Grandmother wouldn't let me get dirty again, not after I'd had my bath. So after much pleading on my part, she let me open up the box of Legos. As long as I was careful not to lose any of the pieces, she said. As long as I promised to listen to everything she said from now on.

I had never had my own set of Legos. I had played with them at the homes of my friends, their Legos sent over by relatives from abroad as well. But in their homes, I was never allowed complete freedom with the pieces. There was a liberty in the phrase "my Legos" that I found addictive, and I said it to myself over and over until I became engrossed with the manual and stopped talking. It contained instructions for building an airplane, not a fighter jet or anything like that but a clunky plane made of squat blocks, with stiff propellers on each thick wing. Still, it was a plane, and they were my Legos. The house had too many grown-up things for me to understand. Legos were simpler.

When I woke up the next morning, Papa was back. But Mummy wasn't with him, and he wouldn't tell me where she was. "She'll be home soon," Papa said. His eyes were red, and Grandmother was staring off at something in the distance. As I walked away, I heard Papa say something about unexpected complications, but I didn't know what that meant. There was a part of me that didn't quite know what to think. Still, Papa had never lied to me. So I went back to my Legos, spending the better part of the day on the carpet, building and dismantling the airplane.

In the late afternoon, Papa and Grandmother sat out on the verandah, sipping sherbet. Papa was wearing threadbare trousers and rubber slippers. He was smoking cigarettes, something I had never seen him do before, and the ashes were clouding the clean-swept floor. There was a heaviness to the air, as though it were about to rain, as if all the humidity was seeping into the house. But the sky was still clear, no sign of a storm. Papa decided that we would go to the beach. We drove there and parked close to the path. It was a broad path, with coconut trees in the periphery. We sat on the sand for hours, a short distance from the water but far enough to see the waves coming in under the fiery disk of the sun slipping into the horizon. No one said a word.

When we reached home, Papa was tired and said he would go rest for a while. Grandmother bustled off into the kitchen, to see about dinner. It was late, later than we usually ate, time we had lost to the sea and the sand. I sat on the Turkish carpet in the living room, cross-legged, playing with my Legos. It was an old carpet, given to my parents by my great-grandfather on the day of their wedding. There were scenes of battle on it, turbaned sultans with curved scimitars directing horses and men in battle. But I took no notice of all this. I was trying to build a house that the manual had no instructions for.

Sabbath

Sundays too my mother woke me up, for mass at St. Patrick's eight o'clock sharp. I never saw her sleeping in. Then breakfast at Koshy's—appams and stew, hot chocolate or Horlick's, a plate of soft buttered toast that we shared. She drove me all around Bangalore in our little red car, guiding us between the darting rickshaws and the heaving buses. She never had an accident.

Russell Market was next for vegetables and fruits—squash and spinach, fist-sized potatoes, mangoes and pears. In back, the pet market with its puppies in cages, lying depressed in corners. She walked me through as I murmured, "I want this one…and this one… and this one…" and walked me out again, her hand on my head.

In her good sari bright yellow and green, and her high heels gold satin and black, she braved the fish stalls oozing with slippery scales, the catch piled high in baskets of ice. Which one shall we make for lunch, she said, and which one shall we fry for dinner? She bargained with the fat butchers in their dark stone stalls—meat slabs glistening on marbled rock, cleavers held in bloody hands. She waited for our bounty.

At home I raced through *Robinson Crusoe* as the smell drifted through all the rooms: fish curry, goat meat, potatoes, spinach and rice. When my mother called lunch, I ran to the table and savored the feast that was her Sunday treat. My father never came. Then, when I was done, she baked quick pudding for dessert.

Bairbre Guilfoyle

Christie Says

(an excerpt)

Christie walked down St. Patrick's Hill, the whiteness of his new trainers catching his eye with every step.

He felt like dancing, like doing a little spin or something, as if he was in a music video and any second now a backing-track would kick in and all the other dancers would spring from shop entrances and the doorways of houses. They'd run over parked cars in perfectly synchronized moves, laughing as they did back-flips over furious Gardaí, who'd chase them on motorbikes that would slide under trucks and wrap themselves around lampposts. Yeah, he could just see it all.

It had been a good day. His da had bought him a load of new gear—a Nike tracksuit (a *real* one – not a knock-off), a couple of T-shirts, trainers and a Nike baseball cap. None of the stuff had been cheap, but his da hadn't batted an eye when he saw the total, just handed over the cash to the fella at the till and passed the carrier bags to Christie.

Turned out the new clothes might have been a bit of a bribe, a way to soften the blow of being told he had to make himself scarce for the evening. His da's friend, Margaret, was coming around to the house, and they wanted the place to themselves.

He'd been living with his da now for over a week and this was the first that Christie had heard of Margaret. But by the shifty way his da was acting and the rising colour in his face, Christie could guess what sort of friend Margaret was. Part of him was dying to get a look at her; see what kind of woman would be interested in dropping her knickers for his da, but the thought of what they would be getting up to was too mortifying. As soon as dinner was over, he'd changed into his new gear and bailed out of the house, leaving his da upstairs, slapping on aftershave and working on his comb-over.

It was embarrassing, really. There was his da—a fat, balding oul' fella—getting his hole, while he, Christie—a young fella in his prime, was left, night after night, pulling his wire to his little brother's old posters of some crappy pop-star. He could swear at this point that even *she* was laughing at him. Things would be different tonight though. Tonight he looked like the dog's bollocks and no woman would be able to resist him. Well, no woman called Tina Buckley anyway.

He'd known Tina for about four years, and, if you were to believe her, he'd fathered a child by her a couple of years earlier. Christie had never shown any interest in the child (a boy), but Tina didn't seem to care and would still give Christie the occasional ride. It wasn't like he fancied her or anything; reckoned she had a face like a bag of spanners, but as his mate Brenner pointed out, you don't look at the mantelpiece when you're poking the fire. And after being locked up for three months, he could poke just about anything.

He turned up Bull Alley and into the gates of the Carlisle Flats. Tina lived in the block nearest the road, but the outer door was locked and there was a dog-eared *out of order* note stuck over the panel of doorbells. Christie wandered around to the back of the block, scanning the second-floor windows, trying to work out which one was hers. The heat hadn't gone out of the day yet and most of the windows were open; net-curtains trailing out onto windowsills. He threw back his head and shouted her name, hoping that her da wasn't around. A couple of seconds later, her head appeared from one of the windows.

"Who the fuck is that?"

"Christie."

"Christie? What the fuck do *you* want?"

"Just came to see how ye are. Are ye comin' down?"

"For what?'

'I dunno. To say hello."

He knew that she knew exactly what he was after, but they had to play the game anyway.

Tina hesitated.

"Me da's out and Lance's asleep. I can't leave him on his own."

"Ye'll just be down here. If ye leave the window open, ye'll hear him if he cries or anythin'."

"Okay. I'll be down in a sec'."

Christie waited where he was, whistling quietly to himself. Things were looking promising.

Tina appeared around the corner a couple of minutes later, pulling on a cardigan as she walked. She hadn't improved in the six months since Christie had last seen her. Her brown hair was now dyed blonde, but a streak of dark roots running down her centre parting reminded him of a badger. A wedge of marbled flesh spilled over the waistband of her tracksuit bottoms, leaving Christie wondering was she pregnant again.

"If me da catches ye here, he'll box the bleedin' head off ye," she said, coming to a stop beside him and leaning against the wall of the building.

"Why? What the fuck did I ever do to him?"

"He doesn't like fellas hangin' 'round."

"The fat little fuck would have to catch me first."

"Fuck off you, slaggin' off me da!"

"Sorry," he said, deciding it was better not to piss her off if he was to have any chance of getting a ride off her. Trying to appear casual, he leaned against the wall beside her, shifting until their shoulders were touching.

"So," he continued after a moment. "Ye're lookin' well. I like yer hair. Suits ye."

"Thanks. Mags is doin' hairdressin' now, and I let her practice on me."

"Yeah, it's nice."

They fell silent for a minute. Tina wrapped her cardigan around her a bit tighter.

"So when did ye get out?"

"Yesterday," he lied.

"Brenner out too?"

"Yeah, he got out last week."

"Well he needn't bother his arse comin' lookin' for Mags. She's got a new fella."

"Has she? He'll be ragin' about that."

"She was sick waitin' around for him."

He nudged her shoulder playfully.

"Bet all the blokes are after ye now, with that new hair style and all. Have *you* got a new fella?"

"Might have."

"That's a pity."

"Why?"

"I was lookin' forward to havin' a cuddle with ye. Kept thinkin' about ye all the time I was locked up." (God, he was going to Hell for this.)

"Really?" (And if you could go to Hell for being a fucking gobshite, she'd be right there with him.)

"Yeah, well ye know how much I fancy ye."

"How come I didn't see ye for months before ye went in then?"

"I was busy with things. Ye know."

She looked at him out of the corner of her eye. He was going to have to make his move.

"So are ye goin' to give us a cuddle, now that I'm here?"

"Well, that's all ye're gettin'. I've got me other things."

(So, she wasn't up the pole.)

"What about a hand-job, then?"

"No. Do it yerself!"

"Ah, go on, Tina. I haven't had anythin' for months."

"Did ye not get yerself a girlfriend while ye were locked up?"

"Fuck off!"

"Or maybe *you* were some other fella's girlfriend."

She was laughing now.

"No fuckin' chance!"

"I thought that's what youse all got up to."

"Who the fuck told ye that?"

Things were taking a funny turn. She kept smirking at him like he was a big joke. He had to get back on track if he was to get what he was after.

"So?" he asked rubbing her arm with the back of his hand.

"So, what?"

"Ye know."

"I'm not bringin' ye upstairs."

"Well, let's nip around to the pram sheds then."

She hesitated for a minute and then seemed to make up her mind.

"Okay, come on. We'll have to be quick though. I can't leave Lance for too long."

"No problem," he said, straightening up and grabbing her arm. He was practically dragging her, but he couldn't give her the chance to change her mind.

The pram sheds were a block of single-story buildings in the centre of the communal courtyard. They'd been built at the same time as the nineteenth century flat-complex and were intended to store the prams belonging to the tenants who lived on the upper floors of the flats. As time went by and lightweight buggies replaced old-style heavy prams, the function of the sheds had changed, and they had become general storage facilities, but the old name had stuck.

As a second-floor tenant, Tina had a key to the pram sheds, and she unlocked the door, glancing quickly over her shoulder as she pushed Christie in ahead of her. Once the door was closed, they were in almost complete darkness, and it was a couple of minutes before Christie could make out Tina's shape in the gloom. It wasn't the first time he'd been in here with her; it was a renowned shagging venue for the local teenagers, but he'd forgotten just how manky the place was. There was no light, apart from the sliver that seeped under the ill-fitting door, and the whole place smelled of cat-piss and mildew.

He put his hand out blindly and pulled Tina towards him, their heads bumping awkwardly as he tried to find her mouth with his. She tasted of tomato sauce and something sour, but he didn't care; it was just good to have someone's tongue in his mouth again. The shed was crammed with junk, but he manoeuvered her around, shifting and nudging until her back was against the wall. Fumbling, he tried to put his hand down the front of her tracksuit bottoms, but she grabbed his wrist.

"I told ye, I can't do anythin' like that. I've got me other things."

"Well, give us a feel of yer tit then," he said, frustration kicking in.

She opened her cardigan and let him put his hand up inside her T-shirt.

"Go easy," she said. "Me tits are sore."

He went back to kissing her, drawing what pleasure he could from her clammy breast, pushing and pulling like a suckling kitten. As soon as he thought he'd get away with it, he took her hand and shoved it down the front of his tracksuit bottoms. As she started to stroke him, he put his head on her shoulder and closed his eyes, breathing in her odour of sweat and chip-oil, as if she'd been standing beside a deep-fat fryer for too long and the stink had seeped into her skin. The hand working his prick was dry; too dry for what she was doing, but he didn't dare ask her to lick her palm. She might get pissed off and stop altogether, and he couldn't risk that.

In the end it didn't matter. It had been so long since a woman had even touched him, it was only a matter of minutes before she was pulling her hand from his khaks and looking for something to wipe it on.

"Here," he said, offering her the end of his T-shirt.

He didn't like mucking up his brand-new T-shirt, but she *had* done him a favour.

Once she'd finished cleaning up and he'd tucked his T-shirt back in, she opened the door of the shed, checking that the coast was clear before ushering him out. As they walked back towards her block, Christie wondered how he could make a swift get-way without pissing her off too much. He was still hoping to get a proper ride off her in a few days.

"So how's Lance doing?" he asked, just for something to say.

"He's grand."

They walked on a bit.

"Do ye want to see him?" she suddenly asked.

"What? Naa, ye're all right. Wouldn't want to wake him up or anythin'."

"For fuck sake, ye wouldn't wake him up just by lookin' at him."

"What about yer da?"

"He won't be home for ages. He's playin' a darts match."

"Better not."

"Ah come on, it won't fuckin' kill ye."

The last thing Christie wanted was to go upstairs and look at a bloody baby, but if he was to have any chance of getting a leg-over at some point, he was going to have to do this.

"Okay. But I can't stay long. I'm supposed to be meetin' some of the lads soon," he lied.

Christie trailed after Tina as she unlocked the outer-door of the block and entered the small hallway. He had been in the building a couple of times before and thought it was an awful kip. Bare light-bulbs illuminated the dank granite stairway, and the whole place stank; a mixture of stale cooking and bleach with an underlying stench of piss. According to Tina, the block was so close to the main gate, passersby sometimes used the stairwell as a toilet. Christie followed Tina up the stairs, trying not to breathe through his nose.

On the second-floor landing, Tina unlocked one of the doors and ushered him inside, putting a finger to her lips to signal that he should be quiet. Closing the door carefully behind them, she stripped off her cardigan and hung it on the back of the door.

Christie had never been in this particular flat before, but the layout was the same as all the others in the complex—one largish room for sitting, cooking and eating, with a couple of bedrooms and a bath-room off it. A counter separated the kitchen from the living room, and a small table was squashed into the corner, barely big enough for two people to sit at. The living area had very little furniture apart from a battered couch and an enormous television-set. A coffee-table sat in the middle of the floor, its surface barely visible beneath a scattering of magazines, teacups and an ashtray. Stacks of clothing were piled on one end of the couch.

He followed Tina into a room on the other side of the living area, almost crashing into her as she stopped beside a large cot just inside the door. As she moved out of his way, Christie found himself staring down at a toddler, flat on his back and fast asleep, a soother lying on the mattress beside his head.

He was bigger than Christie expected. Then again, he didn't really know how big two-year-olds usually were. He hadn't seen Lance for over a year, and even then the most he had done was glance into the pram when he'd bumped into Tina one day.

As he stood beside the cot, staring at the child, he couldn't get over how familiar Lance looked. Then it suddenly dawned on him why.

"Jaysus, he's the fuckin' spit of me da!"

"Is he?"

"Yeah. Me da has that dimple thing on his chin. And see his mouth? And his nose? That's fuckin' mad, that is."

"He's the fuckin' spit of *you*."

"Ye serious?"

"Yeah, even Mags says so."

"Fuck. That must mean I look like me da, too."

Tina shrugged.

Christie kept staring at Lance. He knew Tina had always claimed Lance was his, but since she'd never pushed him for money or any-thing, he reckoned she wasn't that sure herself. Looking at the child now, though, there was no denying it—Lance was his.

Maybe because he was back living with *his* da, Christie started to think it was shite that Lance didn't have a da to do things with him.

His own da mightn't have been up to much but he used to take him fishing and things, when he was little.

"Maybe I should come and see him sometime," he said, more to himself than to Tina.

"For what?"

Christie shrugged.

"I dunno. I could take him to the park or somethin'. Is he old enough to go to the park?"

"Course he's old enough to go to the fuckin' park."

He stood up and scratched the back of his head distractedly. His da had slipped him a tenner earlier and there was a six-pack of beer somewhere with his name on it.

"Right, I better go."

"Okay."

They tiptoed out of the room.

As soon as they were in the sitting room, Christie pulled out his cigarettes and lit one.

"What about me?" Tina asked.

"Shit, sorry, yeah," Christie replied, handing her a cigarette and lighting it for her.

As he put the cigarettes and lighter away, Tina sat down on the sofa and put her feet up on the coffee table, pushing the ashtray and a cup to one side. She switched on the television with a remote control and began to flick through the stations, Christie apparently forgotten.

"Right, I'm off," Christie said, gesturing towards the door.

"Huh?" Tina said, barely tearing her eyes away from the television screen, where a group of celebrities were ice-skating in circles while a smiling panel flashed score-cards at them.

"I said, I'm off."

"Grand. See ye," she replied, her eyes drifting back to the television.

"So when can I come and see Lance?" he asked. He hadn't exactly planned on asking that, but the way she was barely listening to him was pissing him off.

"Don't care…whenever," she replied, sounding equally narked at having her TV viewing interrupted.

"What about tomorrow?"

"What? No! Me da'll be here tomorrow. Wait til Wednesday."

"What time?"

"What?"

Her attention was back on the television.

"What fuckin' time?"

He really wanted to just go over and switch off the fucking telly so she'd have to listen to him.

"Jaysus, I don't fuckin' care! Some time in the mornin'."

"Right, ten o'clock then. Okay?"

"Fine, grand, whatever."

Christie turned and stomped out of the flat, barely suppressing the urge to slam the door. It would have served her right, but he didn't want to wake Lance up just because his ma was a stupid bitch. The poor little fucker probably had it hard enough.

Christine Heath

Path

coamed by Manuka-honeyed iroko teak
this cockpit is the pulsing hub from where
all thoughts and bearings beam
to harbours or horizons or more

wind flows over the curves of sails
and funnels between
seesawing
with the flow of sea
over the curves
of hull and keel

to carve
a groove
that no one
can follow

a sweet
true
path
that
dissi-
pates
in
wake

Thirty-first

It's time to parcel January
in old newspapers
and add it in the compost
with the wood ash

Time to drag warm bones
from the heat of the stove
and seek out green shoots
in the debris under shrubs

Time to trace the ebbing edge
of the roof's shadow
on the south wall
amongst the buds of Montana

Lobster Pot

A southerly squall swoops on the bay
rounds a knuckle of rock
into the strait—funnels
and rushes on.

The red buoy holds firm
in the mouth of the sound
it is drowned in the surge, then rising
cleaves the tide to a rippling V.

Drawn from an oily occult
of gilled things, and heat, and eras
it is tethered to a drama of clawed things
who sup in a parlour on bait.

Fire

beech logs
yield up some
hibernating sun
as yellow licks its
nectar from
the air

beech leaves
who gathered in
those golden rays
are mulched at roots
or suckled into
green

I won't read newspapers any more

I won't read newspapers any more.
I won't let wars flow in printer's ink
through the pupil of my eye
or bruise through my skin
to mingle with my blood.

I'll go outside where the feline air
can writhe and purr in the fine hairs
of my arm. I'll toe the soil
where the foxglove root can
tango with the worm.

On Mullach Cliabháin

Is that a standing stone
and if it is, does it mark some star
the sun or moon
or route across the hills?

Or is an ancient cradled below
who fell – in a dark east wind
his cheek on boggy ground?

And if so: did
water seep downwards then
through turfy earth
to crystallise at zero—
and the fog freeze; and by morning
was the heather blooming white like now
and were the lee sides of icicles furred with frost?

And did sighs from this breathing bog bubble up
and press flat under the glaze
on that shallow streamlet—
their gassy curves moving
in the weave of water?

Or is it just a dreaming stone
scooped up somewhere far away
and dropped
by a careless giant retreating north?

Or, perhaps it's simply not

remarkable at all

in any way.

Triglav Mountain

Slovenia

Snow–melt and rainfall
groove and rivulate your back;
the route is smoothed
by hoofed and booted feet.
Pine and roan roots rise
proud of paths
and search into cracks.

We rise out of woody
and rooty places
to face you,
jagged and sheer and whitish pink;
the way now worn and polished
by boot and hand
and boot and hand.

We climb with you,
our hearts pump hard to follow
fingers feel and find holds
clouds and snow drift below
we are higher now than everywhere.

You take us to you
and as we peak we smile and cry
as though we are the first
and only ones.

From water it came

The unborn paused before birth and fall
and opening wide its half-closed eye
glimpsed a glistening Eden
of peaks patched with ice
and valleys filled with frozen diamonds
cutting a swathe to the fjord.
Old wooden huts on the far shore
haunted by trappers' ghosts
tiny arctic flowers
amid lichen on thawing stones.

Then it looked down and saw itself
in the fresh melt-water below
mirrored with a low cold sun
heard the hard bark of geese
and the sharp cry
of the glacier calving.

Its own sad prolific mother
aching slowly in her rumble downwards.
She watches her child fall
and sail in gleaming splendour out
in the slow flow
to the warmer sea.

Golden Sections

Tiny chickens sucked water from a dish
with an upturned jam-jar reservoir.
She left a bulb lit all night
to keep them warm.
There was a beehive
behind her henhouse
and golden sections
leaked endlessly
in a bowl on the dresser
our busy fingers
scooped the syrup
straight into guilty gobs—
she never noticed.

Her handbag wasn't out of bounds
she never once said it was
it was full of treasures
in secret pockets with zips:
diamond rosary beads from Lourdes
miraculous medals
a powder box with ruby lid
the key to the box under the bed

and loose coins spilled under everything!
We used to tidy these—
she never noticed.

She knitted and knitted and knitted
all us sisters in the same cardigans
she even knitted Frank—
so they said.

It was nearly always Sunday there.
She came to us when babies were born.

emily

all her lines are curves
and every word has a tangent
every syllable's a bugle
every letter an
oh!

Author Biographies

Brenda Collins is from Cork and writes fiction. She will probably regret not having anything wittier to say in her bio for several years.

Melissa Diem was born in New York, lived in Florida, and settled in Ireland at age twelve. Formerly a sculptor, she was awarded a Bank of Ireland Millennium Scholarship in 2002 and completed a B.A. (Hons.) in Psychology in Trinity College Dublin. Shortly after commencing her degree, she discovered she could sculpt entire worlds through writing. Her debut novel, *Changeling*, was published in 2004 by Gill & Macmillan and her second novel, *Ipsi's Trajectory*, is currently with her agent. Melissa's poetry has been published in *New Writing* and the *Sunday Tribune* in 2008, and her poem 'Dreams' was Highly Commended in the Maria Edgeworth Literary Competition in 2008. She is currently living in Dublin and working on her third novel and a collection of poetry.

Rahul D'Silva grew up in New York City and Bangalore, and is at Trinity College as a Fulbright Scholar. He studied English Literature at Swarthmore College in Pennsylvania, where he spent long periods staring at squirrels. While at Swarthmore, he won various awards for creative and critical writing, and co-founded *The Swarthmore Literary Review*. He really wants a puppy, and counts John Cheever, Michael Longley, Chaim Potok, and Wallace Stevens as major literary influences. He would never accuse chestnuts of being lazy.

Nicola Flynn was born in England, raised in Athlone, married in Sligo, wifed and mothered in Tipperary, and has tried living abroad for a while. It is her unshakeable (though so far unfounded) belief that eventually some of this experience will be of assistance to her writing. Apart from that, she has worked as a print journalist, and recently graduated from Trinity College with a degree in English and the History of Art and Architecture.

Declan Gorman is a playwright and theatre director. He is Associate Artistic Director of Upstate Theatre Project, Drogheda, which has produced and toured his Border Chronicles trilogy *At Peace* (2007), *Epic* (2001) and *Hades* (1998), for which he won a BBC/Stewart Parker Award. He also adapted Patrick Kavanagh's memoir *The Green Fool* for a successful touring production in 2004/5 and has been writer-in-residence for a number of rural and cross-border community theatre projects with Upstate (www.upstate.ie) and others.

Bairbre Guilfoyle was born and raised in Dublin. She has a B.A. (Hons.) in English Literature and is currently working on her second novel.

Christine Heath has spent her life so far having adventures and sitting by the fire. She is a nurse and midwife; and when she's not looking after her home, she's off climbing mountains, or sailing her tough little pony-of-a-boat called *Gusto*. She now has a small room with a small stove and she's going to write and write.

Martin Malone is the author of four novels: *Us* (Poolbeg Press—winner of the John B.Keane/Sunday Independent Literature Bursary); *After Kafra* (Poolbeg Press); *The Broken Cedar* (Scribner UK—IMPAC nominated); *The Silence of the Glasshouse* (New Island). He is the winner of RTE Radio's Francis MacManus Short Story Award, the K250 International Short Story Prize and was twice shortlisted for a Hennessy Award. RTE Radio 1 has broadcast three plays, and his memoir, *The Lebanon Diaries*, appeared in 2006. New Island will publish his first short-story collection in 2009. A former soldier, he has served six tours of duty in the Middle East. He is the recipient of several Arts Council bursaries.

Rosaleen Mc Donagh is a Traveller with a disability. She is a graduate of Trinity College twice over, with a B.A. in Biblical and Theological Studies and an M. Phil. in Ethnic and Racial Studies. She has had her play *Stuck* performed at the Project Arts Centre Dublin for Traveller Focus Week 2007. Formerly, Rosaleen worked in Health Education for Pavee Point Traveller Centre and was also co-ordinator of the Violence Against Women programme. Currently, Rosaleen is taking time off to focus on her writing career.

Andrew McEneff was born in Sligo and grew up in Galway and Limerick before coming to Dublin in 1999. He graduated from the American College Dublin in 2003 with a B.A. in Liberal Arts and a year later received his Masters in Modern English Literature from UCD. He is currently working on his first collection of short stories.

Sean Monaghan has published two novels, *Plus Ultra* and *Planned Accidents*, and many short stories. He has completed a B.A. (Hons.) in Psychology and has lived in Thailand, the United States and Canada. He currently divides his time between Dublin and Toronto.

Máirín O' Grady was reared in Co. Kildare. She did three years of English and Philosophy at NUI Galway before moving to Dublin.

Jessica Perreault-Howarth is a wandering Canadian, born and bred in the western suburbs of Montreal. She has a B.A. in Creative Writing from Concordia University, and is currently at work on a novel about death, obsession, language, politics and (ice) hockey.

Erin Rhoda of Washington, Maine received the George J. Mitchell Scholarship to study at Trinity College. The scholarship selects 12 people out of 300 applicants annually for graduate study in Ireland. Erin, a 2006 summa cum laude graduate of Colby College, has been a reporter for the Rockland, Maine *Courier-Gazette*. She is a published poet and writer, with works appearing in Maine literary journals and magazines and broadcast on public radio. Erin was a former president of the non-profit Maine-Ghana Youth Network, which works to educate and inspire youth in the impoverished Ghanaian neighborhood of Kissehman.

Michael Wynne has published both fiction and non-fiction in many anthologies, including *Walking Higher, New Century, New*

Writing, Chasing Danny Boy, QVM2, and *Quare Fellas*; as well as short stories in such journals as *The Recorder, The Saint Ann's Review, The James White Review, Coffee House, Cyphers* and *Force 10*.